The Pulse of Life

The Pulse of Life —
Exploring the Power of Compassion
in Transforming the World:
Essays in Honor of Frank Rogers Jr.

Edited by

Aizaiah G. Yong and Eric Kyle

Claremont Press

The Pulse of Life
©2023 Claremont Press
1325 N. College Ave
Claremont, CA 91711

ISBN 978-1-946230-63-8 (paperback)
ISBN 978-1-946230-64-5 (e-book)

Library of Congress Cataloging-in-Publication Data
Aizaiah G. Yong and Eric Kyle, eds.
The Pulse of Life: Exploring the Power of Compassion in Transforming the World

Dedication

To all those who have taught us the power of compassion and to all those who are committed to growing and embodying compassion with every breath and heartbeat.

Epigraph

"In the midst of the violence that rages around us, music moves through our world as well. This music flows from the very heartbeat of God at the center of the cosmos, and it whispers through every sphere of the universe, inviting each person, each particle of creation, to move in harmony with its restorative rhythms."

Frank Rogers, Jr.
Compassion in Practice: The Way of Jesus

Table of Contents

Foreword

For the last few years, Frank Rogers Jr. has been the senior professor at Claremont School of Theology (CST) in terms of time spent working at this institution. I like to call him our "old geezer" – an appellation which obviously contradicts his energy, passion, and commitment for CST, as well as his role in the ongoing life of this theological school. To be sure, in his over thirty-three years of service to CST, Frank has played a key role in the evolution of our mission. He's been on all the committees at least once, chaired many of the searches, and contributed to several iterations of long-range planning. Although an incredibly productive teacher, scholar, facilitator, and spiritual director, he has never balked at assuming his role in the administrative work that maintains the mission of the school. Frank's contributions to the people and legacy of CST are incalculable; there are many who owe their success here to Frank's generous support in ways known only to them. On a more public level, he has been a source of wisdom for students, faculty, administrators, trustees, and anyone else who has a stake in our mission. This festschrift is an opportunity to hold some of that work to the light, and to celebrate and express our gratitude for those accomplishments. It is likely that for many, Frank's deepest contributions are not written down nor can be shared, and we are grateful for those blessings too.

Frank Rogers started as a member of the faculty in the fall semester of 1989. At the time he was called to CST, Frank was a doctoral student in the practical theology program with a concentration in Christian education at the prestigious Princeton Theological Seminary (PTS). His M.Div. is also from PTS. At the time, Frank claimed specialties in theology (especially Barth and Kierkegaard), spirituality, and Christian education. He taught widely while in graduate school and was also active in local churches. Not surprisingly, he came highly recommended by his mentors at Princeton, though they also expressed their reluctance to let him go. (It seems he covered for many of the faculty there, too.) Frank's primary advisor, the late James E. Loder, Mary D. Synnott Professor of the Philosophy of Christian Education at Princeton Theological Seminary, wrote that he was one of the best two or three of his doctoral students over a twenty-five-year period. Professor of Christian Education Freda A. Gardner considered Frank a person of "superior intellectual ability" who approaches teaching with "reverence and discipline." Another famous scholar at Princeton in Christian education and practical theology, Craig Dykstra, who went on to run the religious grants program at the Eli Lilly Foundation, claimed Frank was the "brightest, most promising young candidate for a teaching position" he knew. Dykstra noted Frank's interest and capacity in a wide range of sub-disciplines, and noted, significantly, that he considered him a colleague. "He has a truly interdisciplinary mind and has committed it to the task of Christian education as a practical theological enterprise."

Frank's mentors at Princeton, and subsequently the CST administration, felt that his religious background was, as one commentator noted, "unusual." There was not much of a Roman Catholic presence in mainline Protestant theological schools at the time, and there probably were not many other Roman Catholic candidates who also ministered in Church of God congregations. Frank's mentors and the CST administration assured the faculty that he was "respected" by mainline Protestants. At a time of denominational entrenchment, Frank embodied a more expansive and ecumenical way of being deeply Christian that communicated the positive values of ecumenicity and religious pluralism. The other challenge facing CST and Frank at the time was that he had not yet completed his dissertation – always a factor of concern when hiring a candidate for a rigorous faculty position. You will be relieved to learn he did complete the dissertation and was promoted from instructor to assistant professor in 1991.

Frank came to his vocation through many streams of preparation. Academically, he attended Anderson College in Indiana, affiliated with the Church of God, where he majored in religious studies, psychology, and the social sciences. From 1977 through 1989, he served as a youth minister, educator, and preacher in eight local Church of God, Roman Catholic, and one Church of Christ congregation. He also worked as a camp counselor, debate coach, substitute teacher, HIV/AIDS advocate, legal researcher, and swimming instructor. (He held some of these jobs simultaneously.) His life experience as someone not from a privileged background equipped him to relate to people across a broad spectrum of humanity, and to meet with compassion those who work multiple jobs, balance family obligations, and face other significant challenges in obtaining an education.

Once a member of the CST faculty, Frank Rogers proceeded to contribute passionately to the curriculum, often teaching beyond the required course load. An enthusiastic academic advisor, his mentoring has inspired countless masters and doctoral students. Vocational teachers are also ongoing learners. Throughout his years at CST, Frank has not rested on the skills he brought to CST from New Jersey. Instead, he has continued to refine his art. From 1998 through 2001 he trained extensively in the dramatic arts with several notable coaches, including Augusto Boal, creator and author of the Theater of the Oppressed. He also served as the director of narrative arts programs for local churches in the Los Angeles area from 2001-2006. Since 2005, Frank has trained extensively as a spiritual director and supervisor, taught in spiritual direction programs, served as a consultant, and developed a private practice. Certified in Internal Family Systems (IFS) therapy in 2012, this work has opened new areas of inquiry and research across the CST curriculum.

After completing his dissertation in 1991, Frank served as assistant, and later, associate professor of religious education until 2002. The turn of the millennium brought new vocational directions for Frank Rogers Jr. He was prepared to leave CST to follow where the Spirit called him. Although enriched by his work as a professor, Frank felt that the Spirit was calling him in some new directions. But the Spirit was also calling CST to come up with a way for Frank to stay. In 2002, the Narrative Pedagogies Project was launched. The project transformed the curriculum of CST. From 2002-2005, Frank continued as an adjunct professor of religious education at CST. He returned to professor status as the Muriel Bernice Roberts Associate Professor of Spiritual Formation and Narrative Pedagogy in 2005 and was promoted to full professor in 2010 – a position he continues to hold on the faculty.

In addition to his programmatic expertise, Frank (as recipient and co-recipient) worked with colleagues to bring several major grant initiatives to CST, thus adding to the resources available to our students and the curriculum. These initiatives include the Spiritual Formation Project, the Narrative Pedagogies Project, and the Youth Discipleship Project, all funded by the Eli Lilly Foundation; the Eco-Justice in Theological Education Project funded by The Center for the Respect of Life and the Environment, The Humane Society, and the Pew Foundation; The Dialogue Across Difference project funded by the Wabash Center; the Radical Compassion Formation Grant funded through the 1440 Foundation; the Cultivating Compassion Through Christian Contemplative Practices funded through Don Morrison; and, the Compassion and Contemplative Practices Research Project funded by the Fetzer Institute.

Frank Rogers has given his all to CST for a generation – there is much more that could be included in this preface. On a personal note, Frank is also majorly responsible for bringing me to CST in 2009. Our family was in discernment about moving to California and I applied for several positions. I was sitting in an airport on my way home from an interview when my husband Paul called and told me that he had an extended conversation with a guy named Frank about CST. He said Frank was PASSIONATE about CST – you can see the mountains from campus – and CST is going to be interreligious – and you can see the mountains from campus – the people are JUST FANTASTIC – AND you can see the mountains from campus! What my husband did not relay to me was that CST wanted me to come for an interview. I had to call Frank, on campus somewhere near the mountains, to determine why he called. But Paul was sold on CST. I have no doubt that if Frank Rogers decided to go into sales instead of religious education, that he would be a wealthy man. Thus, there is some poetic justice that as one of my last official actions as the Dean of CST, I am writing this preface for a book dedicated to Frank Rogers Jr. No doubt the future holds more gracious adventures for Frank, as his vocational path continues to evolve. He has made CST a more passionate, a more compassionate, and a more transformative place!

(The Rev.) Sheryl A. Kujawa-Holbrook, EdD, PhD
Vice President for Academic Affairs and Dean of the Faculty
Professor of Practical Theology and Religious Education
June 2022

Preface

Aizaiah G. Yong & Eric Kyle

Writing a book in honor of Frank Rogers, Jr. has been a collaborative effort full of joy and gratitude. As students of Frank, we have long recognized the tremendous role Frank has played in our lives and were determined to offer this festschrift in his honor and as a small token of gratitude for his service. Spending 35 years in theological education is no small feat and especially all at one seminary! Frank has seen countless numbers of his students' become pastors, scholars, spiritual directors, organizational executives, and international advocates. The fruit of his life is deep and expansive and that outcome is only possible from a person who truly lives out the message preached. And while the vocational trajectories of Frank's students are largely diverse, what they all have in common are the ways Frank's stories, compassion, and dedication have been a support and trustworthy foundation to build upon. We discovered quickly in editing this book that Frank's influence was so wide, we often had to encourage the authors to limit themselves in their reflections on the impacts he has made, and ask them to trust that others within the volume will cover the other dynamic dimensions of Frank's work and thought. We discovered so many creative applications of Frank's influence in the world and continue to be astounded at the good created from his willingness to say "yes" to the invitation of compassion. Thank you, Frank. Thank you for your humility. Thank you for your courage. Thank you for your care. And thank you for being a beacon of hope to all you encounter. We hope this book will bless you and encourage you to "breathe in—the life force pulsating through all Reality" and "breathe out—an expansiveness extended so that all can flourish." And so it is.

Introduction

Aizaiah G. Yong

This book is dedicated to exploring the multifaceted thought and life of Frank Rogers Jr. Frank is a beloved friend, spiritual director, teacher, mentor, and scholar. In loving honor of Frank, the chapters offered within this book explore each of the various roles in which Frank has played to those in his personal life, within theological education, and his leadership as an engaged practitioner of contemplative spirituality in the wider public. While attempting to avoid being reductionistic, it is no stretch to admit that Frank's academic career as a practical theologian has allowed him to harmoniously weave together three major fields which we understand to be the three pillars which most support his work: spiritual formation, religious education, and narrative pedagogy. And, to better appreciate this book, it is important to have a general understanding of each of the core pillars and how we attempted to organize them into three sections. The three sections of the book are: 1) Frank as an educator, 2) Frank as a scholar, and 3) Frank as an engaged spiritual practitioner in the world. In some ways, the key to engaging Frank's work is to consider the following three pillars and to see how they are engaged across the three dimensions of his vocation which the sections are named after.

The first pillar is that of Spiritual Formation and is held together by two main contemplative practices. The first contemplative practice is the Compassion Practice (CP) which was co-created by Frank Rogers Jr., Mark Yaconelli, and Andrew Dreitcer. CP is a contemplative practice that seeks to nurture and promote the presence of compassion within the interiority of the person (and community) who is practicing. It involves four basic steps: getting grounded, taking one's PULSE, taking the PULSE of another, and discerning what to do. In order to fully understand the practice, it is good to note the five key movements at the core of the PULSE steps which are: paying attention, understanding empathically, loving with connection, sensing the sacred, and embodying new life. Each movement deepens the capacity of the practitioner to be compassionately engaged with life as it is, whether through

1

interpersonal relationships or even relationships with institutions and social structures. CP strongly emphasizes that the core of the contemplative practice is to begin with oneself before seeking to engage the outsider world. Rather than seeking to change things purely on the outside, CP assumes that each person will first consider their own interiority and allow engagement with others to flow from there. The second contemplative practice in this pillar is Internal Family Systems (IFS). As Frank is a certified IFS practitioner and spiritual director, so much of Frank's work and teaching explicitly and implicitly integrates IFS. IFS is a psychospiritual contemplative path that was developed by Richard Schwartz and its' core principles are as follows: 1) the human mind is inherently multiple, 2) IFS is radically non-pathologizing and contends that all behavior that is taken by a person is for some reason that seeks flourishing, 3) at the core of each person there is a core Self which is endowed with essential healing qualities such as compassion, courage, curiosity, clarity, confidence, and which can never be fully destroyed. Both CP and IFS are highly influential in Frank's pillar of spiritual formation.

The second pillar of Frank's work is religious education. Frank has long been committed to social justice and passing down the Christian tradition to audiences in the wider public. Frank embraces that religious education happens in both explicitly religious settings but also in settings that are not religiously explicit such as in our schools, hospitals, and civic life. However, Frank is adamant that whether we are conscious or not, we are always being formed. In this pillar, Frank has offered us many ways to become more conscious of how we are being educated and to do it in more life-affirming, inclusive, and expansive ways.

The third pillar is Frank's commitment to narrative pedagogy. Frank is adamant that narratives are ultimately what guide us and carry potential for our greatest transformation. In Frank's work, stories are powerful and they foster meaning, imagination, courage, and agency. The most important question in this pillar is what stories are being told and whom do those stories benefit? How can transforming the stories we tell us move toward becoming more empowered and liberated? Frank responds to these questions by relying upon a narrative pedagogy that contains 6 elements. The six elements he names are: religious literacy, personal identity, contemplative encounter, critical reflection, creative vitality, and societal empowerment. Again, each of these three pillars are important aspects which are helpful to be familiarized with when reading this book as the authors take less time to explain the pillars but to build from creatively through dialogue and critical engagement.

The book is organized into three sections that parallel the many dimensions that make Frank's vocation so profound. The first section explores Frank as a teacher, a wise guide who have devoted himself to passing on what he has learned. The second section looks at Frank's work as a scholar, someone who has made important contributions to theological education and especially the field of practical theology. And the third section considers Frank's offerings to the wider public, as someone who has not remained distant from everyday life but deeply engaged with it. Section one contains chapters from Mark Chung Hearn, Eric Kyle, and Natasha Huang. Hearn discusses how religious education might become a more embodied endeavor through one's teaching. Kyle advocates for the presence of compassion to assist facilitators and educators in their aspirations to cultivate intersectional communities that advance social justice. And Natasha Huang proposes how Frank's narrative pedagogy supports processes related to clinical pastoral education.

The second section has chapters written by Aizaiah G. Yong, Sheryl Kujawa-Holbrook, Joung Hee Kim, and Cate Wilson. Yong considers how the Compassion Practice could lead to a larger renewal within Christian spirituality that is inherently creative, pluralistic, and relational. Sheryl Kujawa-Holbrook rightly claims that Frank should be treated as a practical theologian whose main concern has always been the empowerment of others and their communities of accountability. Joung Hee Kim looks at the traditional practice of walking meditation from Celtic Christianity and considers how the compassion practice strengthens it. And Cate Wilson explores how the practice of compassion can empower women and feminist spiritualities of liberation.

The final section includes contributions by Nancy Fowler, Alane Daughtery, and Andrew Dreitcer. Nancy recounts Frank's role in her personal, academic, and vocational journey as a mentor modeling the potency of compassion in grief and loss. Alane shares about her love for Frank as a spouse and most importantly how he is devoted to practicing in action all that he teaches. And finally, Andrew shares personally about how Frank's life and friendship has supported his work holistically; within his vocation, scholarship through contemplative studies and personal transformation of spirituality at large. The book ends with an afterword from Eric Kyle reflecting on the enormous 35 year (and counting) legacy Frank has made on so many within theological education and beyond.

Our hope is this book will become a vast resource for scholars, educators, and spiritual leaders from across diverse backgrounds who are interested in the power of compassion to change the world. The book admits that contemplation is a deeply personal yet collective enterprise that can only be performed through intentionality, devotion, and reflection. May this book be nourishing and edifying so that the pulse of life is felt once again, embraced, and experienced as the basis of our resuscitation in times of multiple crises and great transition!

Transforming Religious Education through Storytelling, Compassion, and Discernment

Mark Chung Hearn

The puzzled look on Dr. Rogers Jr.'s face when I walked into his office for the first time makes more sense after considering again for this festschrift his commitments, scholarship, and life as an academic-practitioner. He spotted the picture on my t-shirt, a hand-drawn sketch of two Jesuits in cassocks with boxing gloves strapped on. The caption above these sparring foes read: "Jesuit Joust." I would eventually come to know the furrowed brow look, with head tilted back slightly, he was now giving. This inquisitive expression of curiosity shouldn't be mistaken as confusion or disapproval. "What is this about?" he asked. The probing intimidated me, even more so his expression. "I used to coach college volleyball and it's a t-shirt from one of the tournaments we participated in against other Jesuit schools." He nodded slowly; I became even more intimidated. And *that* was my first individual experience with "Frank," the name I, and other students, have come to call him adoringly and respectfully.

"Compassionate life-giver" sums up who Frank was, and is, to me. He was balm to my anxiety as I trudged through my doctoral work. I have come to know that he is a person dedicated to life and compassion, and I suspect the reason why Frank gave a puzzled look when he tried to make sense of the irony in my t-shirt. I am honored to offer a few remarks of reflection and gratitude to celebrate Frank's career and ministry and will do so in Rogerian spirit by weaving together story, reflection, and theory.

Narrative & Storytelling

Anyone familiar with Frank knows minimally the following two characteristics about him. First, narrative matters deeply to him and second, he is an expert storyteller. Narrative and storytelling are inseparable to Rogerian theory, though he might agree that a slight distinction exists between the two. Narrative is an underlying principle of personal and communal identity construction. *Who are we? Who am I?* is often best answered through the telling of life experiences and the relations we hold with ourselves, others, and God. As we tell these stories, the telling builds a cohesive narrative of ourselves and this "core life narrative is the enduring identity that grounds our sense of self."[1] When we pursue questions around who we are, we point to the narrative that holds our identity. We construct our identity (i.e., our grand self-narrative) and bring cohesion to it as we answer identity questions through narrat*ing* and rehearsing self-truths. In this sense, we do not only tell good stories, or "love a good story; we are stories."[2]

Whereas narrative is both the content (i.e., the stories of experience and self-truths) and the meta-culmination of one's identity project toward cohesion and integrity, the way to it is through narrat*ing*, that is, storytelling. Rogers might agree to this small, but important distinction between narrative and storytelling. Storytelling or narrating, is the act of telling a story, though it is much more. Storytelling shapes structure, rehearses the parameters of our identity, and brings vitality to those structures and parameters. Storytelling expresses the idea that we remain a living people who are growing, changing, and transforming, and that the parameters are both formed and fluid. Storytelling is the tool by which our respective narrative, and thus, identity, are constructed.

I have witnessed Frank tell a good story on separate occasions. His animated and engaging style easily draws the attention of the listener. He plays with tempo, rhythm, pause, and inflection. I recall a time when I served as his teaching assistant for an introductory course on religious education. We spent several weeks on a unit where Frank laid out distinctive styles of faith formation: their undergirding philosophy, pedagogical commitments, entry point, goal, and so forth. On this particular day, he was leading the class in a conversation about tradition-centered education and the way our tradition comes alive in us as we rehearse our faith story over and again until that story becomes us. The story moves beyond rehearsal and now animates us. He narrated a memory of his son Justin, playing in the backyard in the sand with his stuffed animals.[3] Justin was "playing" communion and ran out of the elements to

---

[1] Frank Rogers Jr., *Finding God in the Graffiti: Empowering Teenagers through Stories* (Cleveland: The Pilgrim Press, 2011), 57.

[2] Rogers Jr., 56.

[3] Frank narrates this story in fuller detail, *Graffiti*, 62-63.

serve those gathered there. He watched his son think through this shortage dilemma and then brilliantly, think of a different plan, one that would hit at the heart of the Eucharist. Justin grouped those individual Eucharist attenders and rearranged the elements he had given individually to each person so that each table now shared the elements as a group with one another. Frank, as a parent would, beamed as he told this story. You could witness how proud Frank was at both his son's creative problem-solving and at the revelation that the heart of the Eucharist, generosity and self-giving in community, had taken root and was coming alive in his son. Justin was no longer playing make-believe. This story *was* him.

Tears came to my own eyes as I heard Frank tell this story not only because of his skilled storytelling and the ease with which he pulled me and others in, but because this storytelling led to the re-*hear*-sing of this central component in my own life and faith commitments. My Christian commitment came alive once again and my narrative, the structure that gives integrity to my existence, shaped a little more.

Compassion

Two stories epitomize Frank's compassion. After my doctoral course work which took the first two years of my program, my spouse and I were blessed with the birth of our daughter. There is never a perfect time to have a child if one comes across this privilege and gift in life. But my spouse and I thought that if we could plan for a child, the most opportune time would be after course work before qualifying exams (my spouse was also in her own Claremont doctoral program). Little did we know there is no perfect time as hard as we might try. After our daughter's birth, we tried to manage what it meant to live with the joy of being new parents while also navigating the next move in a list of steps in doctoral work. We were spent navigating these steps while learning what it means to be new parents!

I was Frank's teaching assistant and our daughter's birth came right at the beginning of the semester. Physically, the adjustments and the lack of sleep was taking its toll on me coupled with a second, but necessary, job that did not help my exhaustion either. I spoke with Frank to check in about our first class and he said to me unsolicited, "Mark, take all the time you need to come to class." This was the compassion and grace I needed.

In my Korean-American cultural framework, several factors kept me from first reaching out to Frank about taking time off. First, honor one's elders. While my guess is that Frank would not see me as his elder, he was. Professor-mentors are elders in my culture. They are persons who have gone before and bear, and bestow, wisdom on those who follow. They are persons with whom you have a respectful relationship and from whom you not only learn from, but also emulate. To see one as elder is one of the highest degrees of respect one can give to a professor. Second, do all one can to not disappoint one's elders. To not show up to class is disrespectful of the relationship you have with your professor-mentor. If I asked to take time off from class, this might suggest something of what I think about this professor-mentor relationship, or worse, what he might think of me. Finally, education is one of the highest values and commitments we can hold and keep. I admit how ridiculous this may sound given that it was the birth of our first child, but to miss class could cast a cloud over this commitment.

When Frank nonchalantly suggested I take the time I needed to care for my family and myself, I was moved. He saw me. He knew exactly what I needed to hear and did for me what I could not do for myself. As a perceived elder in a relationship with power differential, he made the first move without having to be told to offer it. This invitation was the antithesis of the self-agency and autonomy in which Western higher education and doctoral work is deeply steeped, which is ironic given that the way doctoral work often plays out is contrary to the collectivism about which we often theorize as critical scholars. Frank was living and modeling for me the compassionate caregiving and collective approach to theological education and formation about which he taught and wrote. And in these types of mentor relationships, it takes the one with more power in a situation like this, to do the very thing that is needed for everyone's benefit. I did not experience this invitation as white paternalism but as human compassion from a mentor to a mentee. I saw my absence as two or three substantial weeks missed from a fifteen-week semester. Frank, on the other hand, was being Frank, extending compassion and wholeness to someone in need.

There is another clear example of Frank's compassion during my doctoral work. I took almost nine months to prepare for my qualifying exams when I found myself sitting once again in Frank's office, this time without a Jesuit t-shirt, but with something graver and more serious. I was one month out from my scheduled oral exam, and anxiety was getting the best of me. At the same time my spouse and I relished those joyous moments during the first months of parenthood, we decided that I needed to push through and finish my program so we could secure a full-time job somewhere, have decent benefits, and feel like our lives were moving forward and out from a holding pattern that so often bogs down doctoral students. It was not an easy decision by any stretch of the imagination. My beloved advisor and other dear faculty had moved to different institutions. We also kept hearing of the diminishing prospects of tenure-track or full-time positions in the academy to go along with other institutional challenges such as accreditation probation largely due to financial solvency. It was an unsettling time and now with the added anxiety of needing to finish to support a family, it was a heavy load to carry. Everything professionally felt like it was caving in when I had hoped it would feel expansive and freeing.

I walked into Frank's office, feeling deeply overwhelmed and underprepared for my exams. I couldn't fail my family and the imposter syndrome all but guaranteed I would. I sat on one of Frank's chairs and he took a seat slightly opposite from me. He gave his trademark move, tilting his head back slightly, eyebrows slightly furrowed, and gently asked, "How are you doing?" I shared with him my fears and concerns that I wasn't ready for these exams. He sensed the heaviness of my spirit and in the course of my conversation, said something I will always remember: "These are just shadows in your life. They're there, but they're only shadows and not real." This was again timely balm for my soul.

According to Frank, compassion is the movement "...in our depths by others' experiences and [the ensuing response] ...that intends either to ease their suffering or promote their flourishing."[4] Frank lays out six dimensions of this compassion. These are: (1) paying attention, (2) understanding empathically, (3) loving with connection, (4) sensing the sacredness, (5) embodying new life, and (6) acting.[5]

---

[4] Frank Rogers Jr., *Compassion in Practice: The Way of Jesus* (Nashville: Upper Room Books, 2016), 30.
[5] Rogers Jr., 30-34. One can best remember these six dimensions in the acronym, PULSE with an added reminder to Act on this PULSE.

To truly pay attention is to offer one's deepest awareness and presence.[6] It is a posture of "contemplative awareness" and a move from objectification to human subjectivity. The benefactor of compassion truthfully knows they are seen in their humanity.

To understand with empathy is to be moved deeply by another's experience. The Hebrew and Greek roots for compassion are connected to a person's vital core organs (womb, heart, belly, bowels).[7]

To love with connection is to love acceptingly and with non-judgment. To sense the sacred is to grasp the idea that there is a thin veil between the sacred and secular. Every moment is a moment of the sacred waiting to burst into one's read of a situation. To embody new life is to wish for flourishing in any one individual and throughout all life and creation. Finally, embodying these five dimensions can only lead one to act upon them in goodwill and with the hope of restoration to wholeness. Without this step of action, one might say that a person has yet to fully come into, behold, and embrace compassion.

That day I sat in Frank's office before my upcoming exams, I received deep compassion from him in these wise words that a budding scholar needed to hear. "They are only shadows" provided the respite I needed to soothe and restore my soul and to awaken in me the resilience to move past this stage of my program. It had been an arduous journey to this point, but internally, I was assured through this sacred encounter that I, and consequently, my family, would be all right. Compassion worked in diverse ways for me during my doctoral program, and central to these expressions, was a person who was attentive enough to Spirit, his own life, and the life of the one in front of him. If compassion: (1) holds and heals us, (2) invites us to be liberated from internal turbulence, and (3) invites us to feel genuine care for others then I have known the deep well of compassion Frank personifies and for which I am profoundly grateful and I experienced first-hand.[8]

---

6 The following explanations derive from Frank's descriptions of these six dimensions. Rogers Jr., 30-34.

7 Rogers Jr., 31.

8 Frank Rogers Jr., *Practicing Compassion* (Nashville: Fresh Air Books, 2015), 12-14.

Discernment

Discernment's ultimate hope is aliveness.[9] More specifically, "discernment is the intentional practice by which a community or an individual seeks, recognizes, and intentionally takes part in the activity of God in concrete situations" and "aims at enhancing one's participation in the work of God" and the "healing of the world."[10] Considering the influence Ignatian spirituality has had upon Rogers' own thoughts on discernment, it comes as little surprise that he offers the following three, and important, components to discernment: (1) a passionate commitment to follow God, (2) an attitude of indifference toward all other drives and desires, and (3) a deep sensitivity to the ways and being of God.[11]

True discernment always leads us to participate in the life-giving fullness of God whether that be for ourselves, for others, or for all creation. When our passions, postures, and desires run counter to this, discernment regulates us to the lack of our attention to God. Our misguided attention to wealth, prestige, and security demand a realignment away from these things and a return to God once again.[12] Furthermore, an indifference to these misguided desires, is a precursor to genuine and life-giving discernment. Thus, on the one hand, discernment leads to seeing the misalignment, and on the other, an indifference to these things, allows one to discern even more truthfully to one's current existence and commitment (or lack thereof) to life. One's ability to discern well is predicated upon turning away from the lure of any of these three while one's genuine discernment also allows one to see how these three have taken shape in one's life.[13]

It is possible for discernment to not only go well, but for it to also deceive. When it goes well, it breathes life into the individual

---

[9] Frank Rogers Jr., "Discernment," in *Practicing Our Faith: A Way of Life for A Searching People*, 2nd ed., ed. Dorothy C. Bass (San Francisco: Jossey-Bass, 2010), 103-16.

[10] Rogers Jr., 105.

[11] Rogers Jr., 106.

[12] Rogers Jr., 106.

[13] I suspect Frank would agree that any one of wealth, prestige, and security, either individually or collectively, are not necessarily bad or sinister: one needs a measure of financial resources to live; the best of prestige is respect and admiration; security brings stability. Rather, it is the diminishing and finally, the vanishing, of other values and virtues in one's life, which establishes the pursuit of these three as life-thwarting and, as contrary to life-giving discernment.

discerner or community. Discernment, however, can be misguided and the discernment of an individual or community can lead to destruction and harm. The manipulative leader who fronts as prophet but in turn, usurps power, and often finances, is a case of discernment gone awry. One might conclude though that this action is less about discernment and more about charlatanism. Fair enough but what about a prophet's discernment that is the result of a lack of self- and other-awareness? Though genuine in their intent and action, their lack of self-knowledge and discovery could lead to misguidance and harm. Even more troubling, what about the discernment that comes through honest inquiry and appropriate self-knowledge, and yet is still prone to a damaging end?

Rogers offers six criteria that cooperatively serve as a normative guide for discernment.[14] First, authentic discernment is faithful to scripture and the faith tradition. While this derives from a Christian commitment, it does not preclude those from other religious traditions from also finding wisdom in this criterion. One's religious texts and the other structures of one's faith tradition provides boundaries, both rigid and fluid, to one's belief system. Discernment needs to be faithful to the religious texts and practices of one's faith.

Second, what fruit does the discernment produce? In the Christian context, does the fruit bear the marks of the fruit of the Spirit: patience, kindness, gentleness, love and so forth?[15] If, over time, the discernment and choices made do not lead to this fruit, one might question the original discernment.

Third, the discernment should bring an individual or a community to inner peace, calm, and freedom. If the discerner, on account of the path chosen from one's discernment, is marred by internal strife, by no internal freedom of spirit, and by a lack of inner authority and integrity, then one might question its authenticity.

Fourth, discernment should foster communal harmony. It brings people closer together, and more reconciled and healed in their relationships with one another. This is not to be mistaken as group think or coercion by a few upon the whole but rather, Spirit's work to co-create a communal dynamism.

Fifth, there is a move toward the enhancement, and not the extinction, of life. Authentic discernment points to Spirit's flow and

---

[14] Rogers Jr., "Discernment," 112-114.
[15] Galatians 5:22-23.

wonder, not to a destructive life force. How does one's discernment make one and other's come alive? This litmus question lies at the heart of the fifth norm.

Finally, there is integrity to the process of discernment. A disingenuous process of discernment does not consider alternatives and it does not consider life matters in concert with a faith tradition. An integrous process of discernment is truthful. It aims to seek the truth in a situation and does not cover up difficult, yet honest, information that might be hard to hear but necessary for the wholeness of a person or a community.

In one of the last times I sat in Frank's chair before I completed my doctoral program, I shared with him the discouraging prospects of securing a full-time appointment. I wasn't sure what to do about my future. I finished my qualifying exams, was in the clean-copy edit of my approved dissertation, and now faced the possibility of having no faculty-appointment-pot-of-gold at the end of my doctoral journey. Sure, I could piecemeal adjunct teaching for as long as I needed to, but the thought of this wasn't very life-giving. My life's movement felt more diminishing than enhancing, and I felt a deep wrestling than an inner peace and calm.

I started to apply for positions in athletic coaching and congregational work in addition to the faculty job postings that arose. I attended campus visits for positions in these other fields, even blessed with an offer in some of them. After one coaching interview, I realized in my discernment that I didn't have the drive anymore to coach. My discernment was speaking and before I could notify the school that I was no longer interested in the position, they called to let me know they were going in a different direction and offered the position to someone else. While this further bruised an already bruised ego, the integrity of the process of discernment was working itself out. My interview sure showed that I did not want to coach any longer and now there was one less field to consider. The rejection was the hard truth I needed to hear that brought further clarity to my discernment.

With prospects dwindling, I sat across Frank and shared with him that I was seriously considering going back into church work. I asked him if this was the right move or if I was being too impatient about academic work. I had searched for two solid years which I acknowledge for some doctoral colleagues, is just a hint of their resilient toil they have endured at the job market in theological higher education. Without directly answering my question, he posed a very concrete and wise question: "If you got a church job, would you surf the internet looking for an academic one?" With little pause, I said, "Yes." Frank would go on, "And if you got an academic job, would you surf the internet at night looking to see what kinds of church jobs are out there?" I love Frank's wisdom. "No, I wouldn't." And that was my discernment with Frank about the journey I would take regarding my profession. I would say no to offered church positions, even if our family could have desperately used the security of a salary and benefits, because the truth of Frank's question and the integrity to the discernment process kept calling me to something different in my life.

Over ten years later, I am grateful for that conversation I had with Frank. If discernment leads to aliveness, I received another gift from Frank that day. He helped me come into clarity in a concrete and palpable way ("…would you surf the internet…?"). And while this conversation with Frank concerned my professional pursuits, it would eventually lead to a far greater clarity of vocation in my life, which has brought me further into a deeper internal freedom and genuine authority, all Rogerian marks of an authentic and healthy discernment process. Through my years of full-time teaching and program administration in theological academic settings, I have since come to realize that I am indeed serving the Church through higher education and seminary training. Frank, and his wisdom, was a vital part of this coming alive. In class and in his writings, Frank would often quote Irenaeus, "The glory of God is humanity fully alive." I am grateful he helped me come into this truth.

Implications and Reflections for Today's Religious Education

Before my closing remarks, I want to briefly consider questions and implications of Rogerian theory for religious education today. There are several approaches and philosophies of religious education; Frank lays this out wonderfully in his classes. If I may offer in Rogerian spirit, at the risk of sounding reductionistic, a definition of religious education, it could be this: *Religious education is the work of coming alive to, and on account of, one's held faith and spiritual commitments. Its aim is to help individuals, communities, and societies be healed and transformed from life diminishers into life givers.*

With this understanding of religious education, I raise four areas for further inquiry and conversation: multiplicity, freedom, compassion, and discernment. Multiplicity, a term from postmodern philosophy and narrative psychology, carries the idea that rather than a distinct, singular, self, we each consist of many selves and characters in any given situation or setting.[16] While this idea could be mistaken as multiple dissociative identity disorder, it should not. The strength of this concept lies in its potential for creative resilience. Because life has become so multifaceted and variegated, our many selves end up pulled in different directions while also responding to them. To simultaneously wear the hat of a parent, spouse, employee, colleague, minister, community member, first responder, and the like, all within one person, points to the many "selves" we each hold. We can view this juggling act as the fragmented soul who never feels at home and is always in restless search for one's identity. However, we might also see this as resilience and fluidity. These are not fragments but shards that make up the fuller mosaic of who we are as human beings in a contemporary world. The fact that one can hold all of these responsibilities and identities, and draw wisdom from one for the other, speaks to the integrative work that is at the heart of multiplicity lived well. It is the idea that an athletic coach, church worker, and now, educator-administrator all contribute to the work of what it means to be a faculty member for today's higher education.

A key question to multiplicity is whether there exists the possibility and path toward an integrous life. By integrity, I do not mean, not hypocritical; that is, you do what you say you will do or are committed to, as important as this is. Rather, by integrity, I mean whole, as an integer is a whole number in math. Congruence and cohesion are two related ideas. Is there room today to live an integrous, whole, life amid demanding responsibilities that *can* certainly leave one feeling overly fragmented? While multiplicity can offer strength through flexibility, creativity, and responsiveness, it can also feel like one is stretched thin and left without any core. Flexibility runs the risk of having no grounding, creativity the

---

[16] Cynthia G. Lindner, *Varieties of Gifts: Multiplicity and the Well-Live Pastoral Life* (Maryland: Rowman and Littlefield, 2016), xiii.

danger of being overworked, and untethered responsiveness falling into threatened reactivity.

Narrative and storytelling help the work of viewing multiplicity as gift though they also contribute to its concern. If narrative is the content and the overarching project of one's life, and storytelling is the process that builds one's meta-narrative, it is in keeping with Rogerian theory that we should identify and articulate our stories because the construction, articulation, rehearsing, and retelling of these stories contribute to the building of our identities, and consequently, the integrity of our lives. When we know who we are, with our many varied experiences and stories, we stand more firmly and confidently in *that*, and who, we are.

The caution in pursuing and defining our self-narratives in contemporary society, however, is the excessive turn toward the individual and self. Though there is joy in self-understanding, that journey of self-knowledge and self-becoming may wear thin in a world where we are increasingly awakened to the personal and communal interdependence we have with others. The goal of one's life is not self-discovery or self-agency alone. The goal of one's life is self-discovery so that our agency draws life in oneself, others, and creation.

The concept of internal, interior, or inner freedom continues the conversation. Internal freedom, a foundational principle of Ignatian spirituality, and influential in Rogerian theory, is the idea that one is indifferent both to the external recognition and admiration, and to the internal striving for superfluous things. It does not mean that one is uncaring or dispassionate. Rather, one is not controlled by the pursuit, nor the egoism, that the result of the pursuit can feed. With this understanding, "true personhood is freedom, freedom from the need to secure oneself apart from relationships and freedom from the need to be dependent upon relationships for security."[17] Relationally, one becomes free when they are neither controlled by the need to prove oneself in one's relations nor by the need to prove to oneself that one has no need of relationships. Because one has come into internal freedom, they can enter relationships with compassion and without harm. To come into this place of freedom, honest narrative and storytelling are vital for the reasons I offer in

---

[17] Frank Rogers Jr., "Dancing with Grace: Toward a Spirit-Centered Education," *Religious Education* 89, no. 3 (Summer 1994): 385.

the previous section. However, there is a need for an awareness of the fine line between narrative and storytelling as a project of true freedom, and a project of unhealthy narcissism. For religious education to rightly do what it aims to do (i.e., bring life), narrative and storytelling toward true internal freedom are necessary. Anything less and narrative and storytelling feed into a destructive narcissistic cycle and confirm the reason authentic storytelling and narrative is needed in the first place (i.e., the need for an authentic, cohesive self). Storytelling and narratives of the self are powerful tools of memory, re-membering, and identity construction. However, they can also be used as tools that keep people in deep narcissistic storytelling loops with minimal movement toward inner health and outward concern for others.

True compassion is not only about genuine listening and an interested presence. It is about these and more. It is understanding who is before you, seeing their deeper need, and peering into what actually needs to happen to help this person come to more truthful living. The word attunement resonates here. An attuned person is one who is not only available and approachable, they are also accessible and in tune with what is really going on in a person's life even if that person cannot identify or articulate it for oneself. The attuned person can sense the deeper rumblings of how Spirit is bringing life to a person, even through painful events, news, truths, and experiences. This is compassion, the vitality stirred in one on account of another's own diminishing vitality.

If religious education today is to meet its aim of helping people, communities, and creation come to life, we will need not more proficiency in *techne*, but rather this deeper compassion to which Rogers points. As important as technique is, we need depth that will give meaning and power to it. People know when they have met true compassion. But this kind of compassion and attunement is formed over years; it is not learned in a semester. It is formed in (a faith) community over time and shaped in its leaders equally so. This leads me to a final, open-ended thought, structured in a series of questions.

I interpret a significant part of Rogerian theory as hinging upon discernment: the discernment of Spirit, the internal discernment necessary to do this work truthfully, the discernment of what is really going on in society, the discernment of what is actually being asked or shared by the person in front of you, etc. In our contemporary setting where there are increasingly less persons who are familiar with the traditional "tools" of spiritual discernment (e.g., prayer, scripture, faith community) no matter the faith tradition, how possible is this work? Are we moving toward the discerned wisdom of many individual seekers of spirituality or small numbers of faith communities who carry on this discernment? And if so the former, what do we make of Rogers' criteria for discernment that are in part, based upon both a faith tradition and gathered community? If, on the whole, there is less attention given by individuals and communities to the forming of Spirit in an organized, religious way, how can we develop our capacity to discern, build our compassion, and come to genuine, internal freedom?

If this take on our contemporary religious and spiritual landscape is even partially accurate, religious education needs to consider seriously both its ramifications and its locale. That is, while much discernment has traditionally been centered in the institution of a local church, synagogue, mosque, etc., that discernment now needs different spaces and approaches. Can, for example, conversations about discernment, compassion, identity, and freedom, take place in a CrossFit box, a golf course, in a Bridge club, in a café, or some other place of repeated gathering and commitment and outside any traditional form of Church and organized religion that is familiar to adherents of any particular faith? My answer, and I think Rogers would agree, is "Yes, it can." However, to what extent can these spaces and people gathered do the discerning work to the depth that Rogers suggests? Without the foundational tools of discernment or at least an informed guide to facilitate, it would seem that discernment of this kind suffers from a lack of depth, formation, and wisdom of which Rogers values. Without a basic understanding of scales, rhythm, time, and phrasing, can there be *good* jazz? Similarly, in our contemporary day, the need for an integrous identity, internal freedom, compassion, and discernment are sorely needed. But do we have the necessary tools in place to come into these well? And if not, how will religious education evolve to foster these aspects in those who are less familiar with them and the contexts in which they are traditionally nurtured?

Closing Remarks

Frank, I hope these reflections honor your scholarship and writings and show the deep respect I have for you. More importantly, I hope they provide you with a sense of accomplishment and fulfillment regarding the impact you have had in your teaching and living. You have a long legacy of touching people's lives and for helping to heal the world. Thank you for your kindness, deep wisdom, life posture, steadiness, and gentleness. You have blessed my life and the lives of so many other students. We are so grateful for you. Many good wishes to you as you enter a new life chapter.

Bibliography

Lindner, Cynthia G. *Varieties of Gifts: Multiplicity and the Well-Live Pastoral Life*. Maryland: Rowman and Littlefield, 2016.

Rogers Jr., Frank. *Compassion in Practice: The Way of Jesus*. Nashville: Upper Room Books, 2016.

Rogers Jr., Frank. *Practicing Compassion*. Nashville: Fresh Air Books, 2015.

Rogers Jr., Frank. *Finding God in the Graffiti: Empowering Teenagers through Stories*. Cleveland: The Pilgrim Press, 2011.

Rogers Jr., Frank. "Discernment." *Practicing Our Faith: A Way of Life for A Searching People*, 2nd ed., ed. Dorothy C. Bass, 103-16. San Francisco: Jossey-Bass, 2010.

Rogers Jr., Frank. "Dancing with Grace: Toward a Spirit-Centered Education." *Religious Education* 89, no. 3 (Summer 1994): 377-95.

Intersectional Peacebuilding Through Compassion: Use of the Compassion Practice in Conflict Situations

Eric Kyle

A Muggy Night in Georgia

Yura sits in the empty room, head in her hands wondering what went wrong. Surrounded by scattered chairs and papers strewn on tables throughout the room, Yura's plans for the group were also in disarray. The mugginess of the warm Georgia night seemed to be pressing in and weighing down on her to a point where she could no longer move, no longer breathe.

"What went wrong?," she asks herself for the forty-second time. Things seemed to be going fairly well in the first few sessions, but over time the conversations started to degrade into unfounded assumptions and accusatory anger.

Yura was invited to mediate a conflict at a local church. A Euro-American Methodist congregation had founded the church more than a hundred years ago and had roots in the community as deep as the majestic oak trees of the south. An aging and declining membership had brought them to a point where the members could no longer sustain the old property or its growing financial burdens on their own. Wanting to bring new life and vitality as well as to further commit themselves to the Social Principles of their denomination, they voted to invite a Pentecostal congregation of Honduran immigrants and refugees to use their space.

Almost from the very beginning conflicts began to emerge. Miscommunications and misunderstandings between the two communities were common. Differences in age, religious beliefs and practices, values about family and community, and many other cross-cultural dynamics became apparent each time members of these congregations interacted.

As a trans-woman of color of Syrian descent, Yura understood very well as a seasoned peacebuilder how these intersectional dynamics can affect conflict. Knowing that understanding each of our own social locations is essential for peacebuilding, Yura always strives to help others to increase their critical awareness of these

20

locations. As a result, in her sessions with members from both communities, she sought to help them to realize more deeply how their differences were impacting their interactions and assumptions about one another. Yet, participants were becoming more frustrated and disillusioned the more they interacted.

So, here Yura sat. In the aftermath of a meeting that ended with shouting and misguided accusations. With anguish being exuded as sweat from every pore in her body under the muggy Georgia moon, Yura pondered how she might help these members to better understand how their intersectional differences shape their perceptions of and interactions with one another. She wondered if one of the spiritual practices in her vast peacebuilding toolbox might be able to empower them to better deal with their emotional reactions in healthier and more compassionate ways.

In an instant, Yura's wisdom and many years of experience knew the answer. She would begin to teach these communities the Compassion Practice.

Resistant in the beginning, but committed to one another through Agape Love, members of both congregations allowed themselves to be skillfully guided by Yura in the diverse uses of this practice. Wisely, Yura created small groups with members from each community and led them through this practice on several occasions in both individual and communal ways. By having them share their inner experiences with one another, as well as teaching them conflict transformation processes, over time participants came to better understand how their intersectional dynamics were impacting their interactions and contributing to conflicts in unhealthy ways.

After several months with these members, Yura turned facilitation of these sessions over to a shared leadership team from both congregations that she had been training. With stronger peacebuilding foundations and more compassionate intersectional relationships, Yura felt hopeful for the future of this community as she transitioned on to her next assignment. In her soul, feelings of the muggy Georgia heat shifted from overburdening oppressiveness to a warm embrace of the love that was emerging among these two congregations.

An Intersectional Peacebuilding Aim

In the world of peacebuilding, mediators like Yura often face the intersectional challenges that come with conflict in multicultural communities. For instance, in the book, *Learning the Way of Peace*, the United Nations Educational, Scientific and Cultural Organization (UNESCO) set the following goal as one of the primary aims of Peace Education: "Promote respect for diversities and pluralities in multicultural societies comprising different linguistic, cultural and religious backgrounds."[1] However, engaging with complex diversity dynamics is a difficult endeavor, especially when multiple intersecting identities are present within a group that is in conflict.

Increasingly in recent years, peacebuilders and peace educators have been working to address these complexities by focusing on how intersectional dynamics impact peacebuilding work. For instance, in the book *Intersectional Pedagogy: Creative Education Practices for Gender and Peace Work*, Harmat focuses one of the chapters on exploring how everyday objects are analyzed and interpreted by people from different intersecting social locations.[2] Explorations such as these can provide key insights into how community members, such as the ones that Yura was working with, might internalize and interpret what they are seeing, hearing, experiencing, et cetera in very different ways. These are insights are therefore crucial for peacebuilders working in communities with diverse intersecting dynamics.

So, how can peacebuilders like Yura empower the communities they are working with to become more aware of intersectional dynamics and its influences on how they are engaging with their conflicts? Co-founded by Rogers, the Center for Engaged Compassion *"seeks to repair the world by applying the ancient wisdom of compassion and contemplative practices to the problems of today."*[3] One of the core spiritual practices taught by this Center is the Compassion Practice. This chapter will therefore provide an

[1] UNESCO, *Learning the Way of Peace: A Teachers' Guide to Peace Education* (New Delhi, India: United Nations Educational, Scientific and Cultural Organization, 2001).
[2] Gal Harmat, *Intersectional Pedagogy: Creative Education Practices for Gender and Peace Work* (New York, NY: Routledge, 2020), Ch. 2.
[3] Center for Engaged Compassion, "Radical Compassion: About the Center for Engaged Compassion," Claremont School of Theology, https://www.centerforengagedcompassion.com/about.html.

overview of intersectionality and how these dynamics can influence conflict situations. This will be followed by an exploration of how the Compassion Practice can be used by peacebuilders like Yura to empower communities to engage with their intersectionally complex conflicts in more compassionate ways.

An Intersectional Introduction[4]

In her article, "Mapping the Margins," Crenshaw argues that women of color are intersectionally marginalized when it comes to violence against women.[5] Help for women of color in such conflict situations, Crenshaw asserts, will be limited as many intervention strategies and laws are based on the lived experiences of women from more privileged races and classes. More broadly in society, systemic injustices such as racism, sexism, classism, et cetera are an integral part of U.S. society. For instance, compared to every dollar that white males earn, white women only make 80 cents while black women earn only 68 cents.[6] In U.S. education, when writing about the negative impacts of U.S. policies on Native Americans, Native American scholar, educator, and activist Sandy Grande reports that "in addition to exhibiting the highest dropout and lowest achievement rates, American Indian and Alaska Native students were reported to endure Euro-centric curriculums, high faculty and staff turnover rates, underprepared teachers, limited access to relevant cultural library and learning resources, limited access to computers and other technologies, and overt and subtle forms of racism in schools."[7] As statistics such as these and many others

---

[4] Portions of these sections on intersectionality were adopted from: Eric Kyle, "Addressing Injustice Beyond Justice: Towards Fluid Intersectional Strategies in Education," *Currents in Theology and Mission* 49, no. 1 (2022).

[5] Kimberle Crenshaw, "Mapping the Margins: Intersectionality, Identity Politics, and Violence against Women of Color," *Stanford Law Review* 43, no. 6 (July 1991).

[6] Jaymee Lewis-Flenaugh, Eboni N. Turnbow, and Sharee L. Myricks, "When Intersections Collide: Young Black Women Combat Sexism, Racism, and Ageism in Higher Education," in *Black Women and Social Justice Education: Legacies and Lessons*, ed. Stephanie Y. Evans, Andrea D. Domingue, and Tania D. Mitchell (Albany: State University of New York Press, 2019), 56.

[7] Sandy Grande, *Red Pedagogy: Native American Social and Political Thought*, Tenth anniversary edition. ed. (Lanham: Rowman and Littlefield, 2015), 21.

document, intersectional systemic oppression continues to be perpetuated in U.S. society, centering European cultures.[8]

In an effort to counter such marginalization, social justice activists and peace educators have sought to engage directly with such issues as racism, sexism, classism, et cetera. In my own engagement with this literature, there seem to be several approaches that have been used in response to these injustices, each of which can be used by peacebuilders. The following figure depicts these approaches as a progression from least to most complex approaches. While the order of these approaches may lead us to believe that there is a linear progression from one to the next, it is more likely that different communities may need to utilize one of these more than the others depending on their current context.[9]

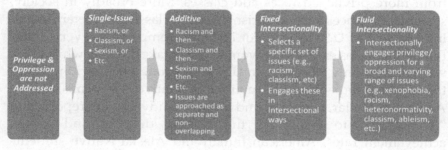

For the first set of approaches, as peacebuilders we can simply choose to *not explicitly address privilege and oppression* in our conflict interventions. An example of this are colorblind ideologies as well as those who claim that they don't "see race" or that they consider oppression to be "a thing of the past."[10] These perspectives can be highly problematic for peacebuilding situations. In their book *Undoing Ableism*, Baglieri & Lalvani explore some of problems of this approach in relation to disability arguing, "In the absence of robust

[8] Susan Baglieri and Priya Lalvani, *Undoing Ableism: Teaching About Disability in K-12 Classrooms* (New York, NY: Routledge, 2019), 31; Barbara J. Love and Valerie D. Jiggetts, "Black Women Rising: Jumping Double-Dutch with a Liberatory Consciousness (Foreword)," in *Black Women and Social Justice Education: Legacies and Lessons*, ed. Stephanie Y. Evans, Andrea D. Domingue, and Tania D. Mitchell (Albany: State University of New York Press, 2019), Kindle Location 144; Keeanga-Yamahatta Taylor, "The Dialectic of Radical Black Feminism," ibid., 320, 324.

[9] I would like to thank Dr. Aizaiah G. Yong for this key insight.

[10] Natasha Howard, "The Reproduction of the Anti-Black Misogynist Apparatus in U.S. And Latin American Pop Culture," ibid., 96.

public dialogue about disability and lack of opportunity to interact in mixed-ability groups, public understandings often reflect stereotypes and misconceptions that compose master narratives on disability."[11] These misconceptions and stereotypes, they go onto assert, further contribute to maintaining existing systems of privilege and marginalization.[12]

As Yura might have encountered in the conflict above, there were likely dynamics of privilege and marginalization between the two communities based on race, ownership of the property, age, positionality in the wider community, citizenship status, and other intersectional considerations. By not openly and directly addressing these, Baglieri & Lalvani argue, community members are more likely to continue act in accordance with existing power structures and thereby perpetuate intersectional systems of marginalization and privilege.

Single Issue approaches focus solely on one issue to the exclusion of other issues (e.g., racism or classism or sexism). The primary focus for peacebuilders with these approaches is to focus their energies on the selected single issue so that significant progress can be made in this area.[13] While such focused efforts may be beneficial for certain contexts, they have also been criticized for failing to capture intersectional complexities.[14] For example, in writing about the experiences of black women in social justice activism, Lenzy reports that "black men are so overwhelmed by the racism they experience that they forget that they also oppress black women" and that black women have had to choose to fight racism over sexism in their peacebuilding efforts.[15] By focusing solely on a single issue, there can be the danger of ignoring other forms of privilege and marginalization that exist within each single issue (e.g, sexism happening within an antiracist movement). In response, some have

---

[11] Baglieri and Lalvani, *Undoing Ableism*, 2.

[12] Ibid., 4-5.

[13] Kim Case, "Toward an Intersectional Pedagogy Model: Engaged Learning for Social Justice," in *Intersectional Pedagogy: Complicating Identity and Social Justice*, ed. Kim Case (New York: Routledge, 2017), 5.

[14] Ronni Mitchell Greenwood, "Intersectionality Foundations and Disciplinary Adaptations: Highways and Byways," ibid., 30.

[15] Cherjanet D. Lenzy, "Navigating the Complexities of Race-Based Activism," in *Black Women and Social Justice Education: Legacies and Lessons*, ed. Stephanie Y. Evans, Andrea D. Domingue, and Tania D. Mitchell (Albany: State University of New York Press, 2019), 264, 270.

worked to address multiple issues simultaneously rather than focusing only on a single issue such as racism or classism or ageism.

In Yura's case, she could choose to help these communities to reflect on how the diverse racial makeup of their community might be impacting how they are interacting with each other. She could lead them through intentional reflection exercises that have them analyze their conflicts through a racial lens as well as to become more aware of their different beliefs, religious practices, et cetera. Such insights could help members from both congregations to better understand one another and directly address dynamics of privilege and marginalization related to race in their mediation sessions.

For *Additive approaches*, peacebuilders might seek to address multiple intersecting issues one at a time in order to help participants have a basic understanding of each of the issues that were addressed.[16] For example, Yura might begin by working with the group on analyzing their conflict through the lens of racism and then move onto sexism, followed by classism, et cetera. In such approaches, these intersectional issues are treated as separate and distinct aspects of privilege and oppression in the conflict. However, such additive approaches are asserted by some to be problematic because they can tend to erase the experiences of those living at the intersection of multiple marginalized social locations simultaneously,[17] as we have already learned from Crenshaw above. These approaches also ignore the marginalization that occurs within each category, also noted above (e.g, sexism happening within an antiracist movement).

In response, and building on previous scholars and practitioners, Crenshaw wrote a series of seminal articles calling for intersectional methods of analyses and engagement that center the lived experiences of multiple intersecting social locations.[18] Intersectionality therefore seeks to decenter current "norms," which

---

[16] Patrick R. Grzanka, "Undoing the Psychology of Gender: Intersectional Feminism and Social Science Pedagogy," in *Intersectional Pedagogy: Complicating Identity and Social Justice*, ed. Kim Case (New York: Routledge, 2017), 66.

[17] Kim A. Case, "Toward an Intersectional Pedagogy Model: Engaged Learning for Social Justice," ibid., ed. Kim A. Case (New York, NY), 2; Greenwood, "Intersectionality Foundations and Disciplinary Adaptations," 28.

[18] Case, "Toward an Intersectional Pedagogy Model," 2; Ursula Moffitt, Linda P. Juang, and Moin Syed, "Intersectionality and Youth Identity Development Research in Europe," *Frontiers in Psychology* 11 (2020).

are being used to perpetuate oppression,[19] by recentering multiple alternative social locations. In what I term *"Fixed Intersectionality,"* peacebuilders would choose a fixed set of social locations to focus on. Some of the most commonly addressed forms of oppression are racism, sexism, classism, ableism, ageism, and heteronormativity.[20]

So, for instance, Yura might choose to focus on race, property ownership, and immigration status, helping both congregations to better understand how these might be combining to create privilege and marginalization dynamics that might be negatively impacting their ability to work through their conflicts. Following intersectional theorist and activists, she might work with this community to help them to decenter white, property owning, U.S. citizen culture and create more inclusiveness and empowerment for other social locations. As intersectional experts Evans, Domingue, and Mitchell explain, "By decentering maleness and whiteness, questions of justice at once solidify intersectional analyses and moves discussion out of locations traditionally represented as normative."[21] These approaches have shown positive effects on human development by educational researchers, with Case reporting that "intersectional awareness was negatively associated with justification for gender and race inequalities and endorsement of a powerful group's

---

[19] Bettina L. Love and Sarah Abdelaziz, "We Got a Lot to Be Mad About: A Seat at Solange's Table," in *Black Women and Social Justice Education: Legacies and Lessons,* ed. Stephanie Y. Evans, Andrea D. Domingue, and Tania D. Mitchell (Albany: State University of New York Press, 2019), 165.

[20] Robin Brooks, "Black, Female, and Teaching Social Justice: Transformative Pedagogy for Challenging Times," ibid., 186; Keffrelyn D. Brown, "Effectively Teaching the One Course on Race and Culture: Critical Explorations from a Black Woman Social Justice Teacher Educator," ibid., 233, 236-238; Grande, *Red Pedagogy,* 193; Tugce Kurtis and Glenn Adams, "Decolonial Intersectionality: Implications for Theory, Research, and Pedagogy," in *Intersectional Pedagogy: Complicating Identity and Social Justice,* ed. Kim Case (New York: Routledge/Taylor & Francis Group ,, 2017), 47; Lenzy, "Navigating the Complexities of Race-Based Activism," 272-273; Lewis-Flenaugh, Turnbow, and Myricks, "When Intersections Collide," 63; Tania Mitchell, "Gone Missin': The Absence of Black Women's Praxis in Social Justice Theory," ibid., 38; Nancy A. Naples, "Pedagogical Practice and Teaching Intersectionality Intersectionally," in *Intersectional Pedagogy: Complicating Identity and Social Justice,* ed. Kim Case (New York: Routledge, 2017), 114.

[21] Stephanie Y. Evans, Andrea D. Domingue, and Tania D. Mitchell, "Introduction: Black Women's Educational and Social Justice Values of the 94 Percent," in *Black Women and Social Justice Education: Legacies and Lessons,* ed. Stephanie Y. Evans, Andrea D. Domingue, and Tania D. Mitchell (Albany: State University of New York Press, 2019), 2.

dominance over out-groups."[22] As it relates to Yura's situation, working with the community to de-center traditionally dominating social locations (e.g., white, male, etc.) can open up possibilities for different healthy ways of viewing and engaging with conflicts.

As with the previous approaches, there are limits to Fixed Intersectional approaches. The most obvious one is the question of how a peacebuilder can engage with multitudinous and diverse intersecting social locations that shape identity and can be the basis for marginalization and privilege. For example, a search for "diversity identity wheel" on the internet will reveal images that depict numerous aspects of an individual's social location that can affect their identity. An example of this is the United Way's model that contains no less than 39 different factors that can be used to define one's intersectional social location.[23] For the Fixed Intersectional approaches, if we select only a subset of these social locations to focus on, most of these other social locations would likely go unexplored and may continue to contribute to marginalization and privilege in peacebuilding processes.

Towards Fluid Intersectional Approaches

Given the aims of peacebuilding to "Promote respect for diversities and pluralities in multicultural societies comprising different linguistic, cultural and religious backgrounds" as well as the challenges that intersectional dynamics can contribute to complex conflicts, how might peacebuilders and peace educators respond? We have already explored ways that Yura might help members of both congregations to develop their intersectional competencies and thereby address their conflicts in healthier ways. Yet, each of the approaches above has limits that need to be addressed.

So, how might we respond? Drawing primarily from intersectional social justice education literature, there are at least four sets of *"Fluid Intersectional"* strategies that can be used to support intersectional engagement and development in peacebuilding. This section will briefly outline each of these approaches while the final section of this chapter will explore how

---

[22] Case, "Toward an Intersectional Pedagogy Model," 6-7.
[23] "Diversity, Equity and Inclusion," United Way of Asheville and Buncombe County, https://www.unitedwayabc.org/diversity-equity-and-inclusion.

28

Yura's use of the Compassion Practice may have embodied each of these.

The first set of strategies is *helping participants to explore their own and one another's intersecting social locations* along with diverse intersectional locations in society more broadly. For participants and peacebuilders alike, the importance of knowing one's own social location is asserted to be central for intersectional development.[24] Examples of this strategy include having participants develop autobiographical cases as well as to reflect on their own hidden assumptions and biases. These can help to foster greater awareness of their own unique intersecting social locations.[25] Participants are also to explore diverse and multiple social locations of others, particularly those from non-privileged locations (e.g., non-white, non-male, non-middle/upper class, etc.).[26] One of the primary goals of these Fluid Intersectional strategies is to continually "shake up" and disrupt the stereotypes that are associated with specific, but more widely varying, intersecting social locations.[27] By exploring the lived experiences of multiple and diverse intersecting social locations, participants can more fluidly learn how marginalization and privilege impact specific persons and communities during conflict situations.[28]

---

[24] Brooks, "Black, Female, and Teaching Social Justice," 184; Adrienne Dessel and Timothy Corvidae, "Experiential Activities for Engaging Intersectionality in Social Justice Pedagogy," in *Intersectional Pedagogy: Complicating Identity and Social Justice,* ed. Kim Case (New York: Routledge, 2017), 221; Naomi M. Hall, "Quotes, Blogs, Diagrams, and Counter-Storytelling: Teaching Intersectionality at a Minority-Servicing Institution," ibid., 157; Chrystal A. George Mwangi and Keisha L. Green, "Reflections on Moving Theory to Praxis: Dialectical Engagements of Black Women Faculty in an Urban High School Space," in *Black Women and Social Justice Education: Legacies and Lessons,* ed. Stephanie Y. Evans, Andrea D. Domingue, and Tania D. Mitchell (Albany: State University of New York Press, 2019), 286; Jennifer Steele, "Acknowledging Diversity in the Classroom," in *Learning to Teach for Social Justice,* ed. Linda Darling-Hammond, Jennifer French, and Silvia Paloma García-Lopez (New York: Teachers College Press, 2002), 20.
[25] Brown, "Effectively Teaching the One Course on Race and Culture," 238, 239; Grzanka, "Undoing the Psychology of Gender," 71, 75.
[26] Brooks, "Black, Female, and Teaching Social Justice," 184.
[27] Michelle R. Dunlap, Christina D. Burrell, and Penney Jade Beaubrun, "Moments in the Danger Zone: Encountering "Non-Racist," "Non-Racial," "Non-Color-Seeing," Do-Gooders," ibid., 202.
[28] Grzanka, "Undoing the Psychology of Gender," 66.

A second set of strategies that are recommended builds upon the first set. In addition to focusing on specific and varying case examples of marginalization and privilege, *participants are also to learn more generally about how systems of oppression operate and the wider effects that they have in society.*[29] It is here that Single-Issue approaches can be helpful for understanding how local and societal systems embody and perpetuate specific forms of oppression and privilege. However, to counter the negative effects of Single-Issue, Additive, and Fixed Intersectional approaches, such analyses should also be engaged within a more broadly diverse and fluid intersectional framework. They can note, for instance, that within race-based conflicts there can also sexist, classist, ableist, et cetera forms of oppression.[30] When multiple and diverse combinations of analyses are applied (e.g., combining heteronormativity analyses with other types of analyses, such as classism, nationalism, etc.), participants can learn to integrate and fluidly apply these various tools of systemic critical analysis based on their unique situation.

As Banks highlights in his theory of Multicultural Education, approaches that theoretically explore and critically reflect on diverse perspectives is not enough. Peacebuilding and peace education should also empower participants, Banks asserts, to "pursue projects and activities that allow them to make decisions and to take personal, social, and civic actions related to the concepts, problems, and issues they have studied."[31] *Engaging in social action* is therefore a third set of strategies that are recommended for Fluid Intersectional approaches.[32] Overall, a goal of these strategies is to help participants to enact real structural change for the people, communities, and systems that they are connected to and that are

---

[29] Brooks, "Black, Female, and Teaching Social Justice," 186; Michele D. Smith and Maia Niguel Moore, "Black Feminist Thought: A Response to White Fragility," ibid., 85-87.

[30] Mitchell, "Gone Missin'," 38.

[31] James A. Banks, *An Introduction to Multicultural Education*, Fourth ed. (Boston, MA: Pearson Education, 2008), 49.

[32] Andrea D. Domingue and Stephanie Evans, "Concluding Thoughts: Black Women Educators, Healing History, and Developing a Sustainable Social Justice Practice," in *Black Women and Social Justice Education: Legacies and Lessons*, ed. Stephanie Y. Evans, Andrea D. Domingue, and Tania D. Mitchell (Albany: State University of New York Press, 2019), 344; Grzanka, "Undoing the Psychology of Gender," 67; Lenzy, "Navigating the Complexities of Race-Based Activism," 272-273.

impacting the conflicts they are having.[33] When varying and multiple intersectional analyses are applied to this social action work, participants can learn to engage in ways that address the wider social, political, and economic systems that are influencing their conflicts in negative ways.

A final set of strategies are those that *provide close support as well as systems of solidarity and allyship for participants, particularly those from marginalized social locations.*[34] Such support systems should be intentionally anti-oppressive, seeking to counter the negative impact of whitestream systems[35] for both marginalized and privileged participants.[36] Such strategies require that they personally experience the peacebuilding processes as a safe space and that they are free to share their ideas and perspectives.[37] They can also include close mentoring to help participants from marginalized backgrounds to build social capital, break patterns of internalized oppression, develop coping mechanism for oppressive situations, and increase access to additional services and support systems.[38] Through these complex interactions and support systems, participants can engage in meaningful ways with diverse intersecting social locations, thereby countering the negative effects of intersectional marginalization in the peacebuilding process.

Intersectional Peacebuilding Through Compassion

In the section introducing intersectional strategies, from not addressing diversity at all to Fixed Intersectional approaches, we explored how Yura might have used each one of these. However, each of these has limits to their applications. In her wisdom, Yura elected to use the Compassion Practice to help the two congregations develop their fluid intersectional capacities and thereby deal with their cross-cultural conflicts in healthier ways. In this final section, following the Fluid Intersectional strategies from

---

[33] Grande, *Red Pedagogy*, 5, 242.

[34] Lenzy, "Navigating the Complexities of Race-Based Activism," 272-273.

[35] This term was adapted from Grande, who defines this as "white, middle class" culture. Grande, *Red Pedagogy*, 181.

[36] Love and Abdelaziz, "We Got a Lot to Be Mad About," 177.

[37] Brooks, "Black, Female, and Teaching Social Justice," 195-196.

[38] Brenda L. H. Marina, "Social Conceptions and the Angst of Mentoring Women of Diverse Backgrounds in Higher Education," ibid., 246-253.

the previous section, we will explore how the Compassion Practice might have been used by Yura to achieve these ends.

In their paper, "Contemplative Race Theory," Cohen and Carter explore the use of the Compassion Practice to help teach about race and racism.[39] Being focused primarily on race, a Single-Issue approach, Carter provides valuable insights into how the Compassion Practice empowered him to deal with his frustrations and disappointments as a black male experiencing marginalization in predominantly white institutions. As it has been developed by the Center for Engaged Compassion, Carter outlines the following steps for the Compassion Practice:

1. Anchoring: This step fosters a grounded, non-reactive, non-judgmental space that the practitioner can dwell in and return to if needed throughout the practice. Anchoring is used to create this space via focusing on one's breath, the weightiness of one's body, or imagining oneself in a space that elicits feelings of safety, compassion, or sacredness.

2. Beholding: From this grounded space practitioners are invited to notice the presence of difficult feelings or negative voices which are then imaginally placed in a separate space where they can be observed and examined. Beholding fosters a sense of open curiosity, and allows interior freedom to emerge.

3. Connecting: Deepens one's experience with the feeling or voice being examined through an imaginal process of personifying it, usually as a small misunderstood child. This enables the practitioner to converse with the feeling or voice and allows a relationship with him or her to emerge. The process of connecting fosters empathic care, compassion, wisdom about what the feeling or voice needs, and the beginnings of interior freedom toward the feeling or voice being examined.

4. Dwelling: As the feeling or voice becomes more understood and a sense of compassion begins to grow, practitioners are now encouraged to invite the source of that compassion to engage the child as well as themselves in a healing and restorative way. Dwelling fosters interior freedom, a widening sense of interior

---

[39] Seth Schoen and Christopher Carter, "Contemplative Race Theory," in *Association for Contemplative Mind in Higher Education (ACMHE)* (Amherst, MA2013).
http://www.contemplativemind.org/files/ConRaceTheory_PUB_Draft.pdf

stillness, an experience of communion or union, and an encompassing feeling of compassion.

5. Embracing your Restored Self: In the penultimate step of the compassion practice participants are asked to notice what grace they are receiving within it and to let it soak into them and claim it as a living part of who they are. This step fosters interior stability, wisdom, and a new experiential awareness of one's reality.

6. Freely Discerning Compassionate Action: From this state of compassion and in-dwelling grace practitioners are guided to shift their attention to the original feeling or voice with which they began the practice. Beholding it with empowered compassion they are invited to sense within themselves a way to engage that feeling or voice that embodies the compassion and grace they have experienced during the practice. This final step turns empathy and wisdom into empowered compassionate action or behavior.

In these steps, we can find resonances with the Fluid Intersectional approaches described in the previous section. Given these approaches, how might Yura have skillfully used the Compassion Practice to help the two congregations develop their intersectional capacities and thereby engage in peacebuilding processes in more productive ways? We will explore the use of the Compassion Practice not only for individuals engaging with this practice (i.e., an inner, reflective contemplative practice) but also using these steps as a guide for communal practices and conflict transformation activities.

For Anchoring, individuals in the two congregations can seek to center themselves and better enter into conversations with one another from a place of grounding love. Yura can also seek to anchor this community in love by having them establish ground rules and engage with other conflict transformation activities that help to establish a safe space for all participants. What is important in both of these individual and communal practices, from a Fluid Intersectional perspective, is to help participants establish a safe space where differences, tolerance, and openness to diverse perspectives is normed. In doing so, Yura would be working to create the beginnings of systems of solidarity and allyship for participants. This step of the Compassion Practice therefore seeks to establish a strong foundation and environment for fluid intersectional engagement with conflict transformation processes.

Following the Beholding step, Yura might lead individuals in the Compassion Practice to help them reflect on their own personal engagement with the conflicts they are experiencing. As they engage with these inner reflections, they could be invited to note negative biases, stereotypes, assumptions, et cetera that are emerging within them based on others' intersectional identities (e.g., stereotypes about women, immigrants, upper class persons, etc.). As a community, Yura could also guide them through discussions that help them to name these common intersectional biases and reflect on how they might be affecting the relationships and conflicts between the two congregations. What is important, intersectionally, is ensuring that participants consider a wide range of diverse yet specific intersecting identities. In doing so, Yura would be helping participants to explore their own and one another's intersecting social locations and how these can fluidly impact conflicts. The Beholding step is therefore an essential part of empowering these congregations to enter more deeply into the sources of their conflicts in fluid intersectional ways.

Following the Compassion Practice's next major movement, Connecting, Yura would continue to encourage participants to reflect ever more deeply on their own and one another's biases, through both inner contemplative reflections as well as via large and small group activities. The processes of personifying these intersectional biases and their influences on conflict should help to lead individuals and these congregations to deeper levels of empathy and compassion for themselves and each other. By connecting more deeply with the fears, hopes, et cetera that underlie these negative intersecting biases, group members can better understand their own and one another's behaviors. This is also an opportunity to more clearly perceive the intersectional diversity of experiences, beliefs, practices, and values that exist within and across each congregation. Furthermore, such activities can help them to understand how wider social, political, and economic systems of oppression and power can affect their interactions and perspectives in positive and negative ways. Through these Connecting processes, Yura is therefore helping this community to both expand and deepen their intersectional peacebuilding capacities.

As this community transitions towards and through the Dwelling step, Yura would help them to draw more deeply on their images, experiences, and beliefs about the Sacred. Individually, participants seek to interact with the Sacred within themselves, allowing any movements of healing, insights of wisdom, invitations to transformation, et cetera to emerge. As a community, Yura might empower these congregations to engage in rituals and practices of restoration, healing, and community building. Following participatory processes, these individual and communal activities should be diverse, empowering intersectional expression of various social locations. Doing so can help these congregations to deepen their systems of support and allyship as this community learns together how to heal, restore, and transform their conflicts in intersectional ways.

By Dwelling in these healing processes, Yura can help this more unified community to Embrace restored and newer visions of themselves, one another, and their congregations as a whole. As individuals, participants can clarify healthier versions of their intersectional identities. As a community, they can brainstorm how they would more ideally like to be in relationship with one another as their congregations draw closer together. Out of these reflections, Yura might lead this community to set goals that they would like to aspire to, discuss healthier peacebuilding processes, et cetera that are more inclusive of the intersecting social locations that are present within both congregations. Overall, Yura would be helping this community to Embrace healthier versions of themselves and each other, which then leads into the final step of the Compassion Practice.

By discerning and pursuing Compassionate Action, Yura is empowering these congregations to embody the many transformations that the previous steps have been fostering. Individually, participants can commit themselves to living in substantively different ways, particularly with how they intersectionally react to and engage with conflicts. As a community, Yura would help these congregations to develop intersectionally appropriate peacebuilding processes that are continually modified as their community changes. She could also help them to develop plans for engaging in social action that seeks to transform the wider societal systems of privilege and marginalization that are negatively impacting their community members. In this final step, Yura could work with this community to enact intersectional peacebuilding

35

processes and activities that fosters greater compassion and healing both within and beyond their congregations.

Epilogue...

As Yura moves on to her next important assignment, members of the community that she worked with are left with a valuable spiritual practice and peacebuilding processes. Thanks to Yura, they are continuing to grow in their intersectional capacities. These capacities, as UNESCO highlights, are essential aims to be pursued amidst all peace education and peacebuilding initiatives. The Compassion Practice, as we have learned in this chapter, is a helpful practice to utilize with both individuals and communities as a whole, along with many others in the peacebuilders' toolbox. When used wisely, as Yura did, it can empower communities in conflict to further achieve intersectional peace through compassion.

Bibliography

Baglieri, Susan, and Priya Lalvani. *Undoing Ableism: Teaching About Disability in K-12 Classrooms.* New York, NY: Routledge, 2019.

Banks, James A. *An Introduction to Multicultural Education.* Fourth ed. Boston, MA: Pearson Education, 2008.

Brooks, Robin. "Black, Female, and Teaching Social Justice: Transformative Pedagogy for Challenging Times." In *Black Women and Social Justice Education: Legacies and Lessons*, edited by Stephanie Y. Evans, Andrea D. Domingue and Tania D. Mitchell, 183-200. Albany: State University of New York Press, 2019.

Brown, Keffrelyn D. "Effectively Teaching the One Course on Race and Culture: Critical Explorations from a Black Woman Social Justice Teacher Educator." In *Black Women and Social Justice Education: Legacies and Lessons*, edited by Stephanie Y. Evans, Andrea D. Domingue and Tania D. Mitchell, 231-244. Albany: State University of New York Press, 2019.

Case, Kim. "Toward an Intersectional Pedagogy Model: Engaged Learning for Social Justice." In *Intersectional Pedagogy: Complicating Identity and Social Justice*, edited by Kim Case, 1-24. New York: Routledge, 2017.

Case, Kim A. "Toward an Intersectional Pedagogy Model: Engaged Learning for Social Justice." In *Intersectional Pedagogy:*

Complicating Identity and Social Justice, edited by Kim A. Case, 1-24. New York, NY: Routledge, 2017.

Center for Engaged Compassion. "Radical Compassion: About the Center for Engaged Compassion." Claremont School of Theology, https://www.centerforengagedcompassion.com/about.html.

Crenshaw, Kimberle. "Mapping the Margins: Intersectionality, Identity Politics, and Violence against Women of Color." *Stanford Law Review* 43, no. 6 (July 1991): 1241-1299.

Dessel, Adrienne, and Timothy Corvidae. "Experiential Activities for Engaging Intersectionality in Social Justice Pedagogy." In *Intersectional Pedagogy: Complicating Identity and Social Justice*, edited by Kim Case, 214-231. New York: Routledge, 2017.

"Diversity, Equity and Inclusion." United Way of Asheville and Buncombe County, https://www.unitedwayabc.org/diversity-equity-and-inclusion.

Domingue, Andrea D., and Stephanie Evans. "Concluding Thoughts: Black Women Educators, Healing History, and Developing a Sustainable Social Justice Practice." In *Black Women and Social Justice Education: Legacies and Lessons*, edited by Stephanie Y. Evans, Andrea D. Domingue and Tania D. Mitchell, 341-352. Albany: State University of New York Press, 2019.

Dunlap, Michelle R., Christina D. Burrell, and Penney Jade Beaubrun. "Moments in the Danger Zone: Encountering "Non-Racist," "Non-Racial," "Non-Color-Seeing," Do-Gooders." In *Black Women and Social Justice Education: Legacies and Lessons*, edited by Stephanie Y. Evans, Andrea D. Domingue and Tania D. Mitchell, 201-218. Albany: State University of New York Press, 2019.

Evans, Stephanie Y., Andrea D. Domingue, and Tania D. Mitchell. "Introduction: Black Women's Educational and Social Justice Values of the 94 Percent." In *Black Women and Social Justice Education: Legacies and Lessons*, edited by Stephanie Y. Evans, Andrea D. Domingue and Tania D. Mitchell, 1-20. Albany: State University of New York Press, 2019.

Grande, Sandy. *Red Pedagogy: Native American Social and Political Thought.* Tenth anniversary edition. ed. Lanham: Rowman and Littlefield, 2015.

Greenwood, Ronni Mitchell. "Intersectionality Foundations and Disciplinary Adaptations: Highways and Byways." In

Intersectional Pedagogy: Complicating Identity and Social Justice, edited by Kim Case, 27-45. New York: Routledge, 2017.

Grzanka, Patrick R. "Undoing the Psychology of Gender: Intersectional Feminism and Social Science Pedagogy." In *Intersectional Pedagogy: Complicating Identity and Social Justice*, edited by Kim Case, 63-81. New York: Routledge, 2017.

Hall, Naomi M. "Quotes, Blogs, Diagrams, and Counter-Storytelling: Teaching Intersectionality at a Minority-Servicing Institution." In *Intersectional Pedagogy: Complicating Identity and Social Justice*, edited by Kim Case, 150-170. New York: Routledge, 2017.

Harmat, Gal. *Intersectional Pedagogy: Creative Education Practices for Gender and Peace Work*. New York, NY: Routledge, 2020.

Howard, Natasha. "The Reproduction of the Anti-Black Misogynist Apparatus in U.S. And Latin American Pop Culture." In *Black Women and Social Justice Education: Legacies and Lessons*, edited by Stephanie Y. Evans, Andrea D. Domingue and Tania D. Mitchell, 91-102. Albany: State University of New York Press, 2019.

Kurtis, Tugce, and Glenn Adams. "Decolonial Intersectionality: Implications for Theory, Research, and Pedagogy." In *Intersectional Pedagogy: Complicating Identity and Social Justice*, edited by Kim Case, 46-59. New York: Routledge/Taylor & Francis Group ,, 2017.

Kyle, Eric. "Addressing Injustice Beyond Justice: Towards Fluid Intersectional Strategies in Education." *Currents in Theology and Mission* 49, no. 1 (2022): 44-50.

Lenzy, Cherjanet D. "Navigating the Complexities of Race-Based Activism." In *Black Women and Social Justice Education: Legacies and Lessons*, edited by Stephanie Y. Evans, Andrea D. Domingue and Tania D. Mitchell, 261-274. Albany: State University of New York Press, 2019.

Lewis-Flenaugh, Jaymee , Eboni N. Turnbow, and Sharee L. Myricks. "When Intersections Collide: Young Black Women Combat Sexism, Racism, and Ageism in Higher Education." In *Black Women and Social Justice Education: Legacies and Lessons*, edited by Stephanie Y. Evans, Andrea D. Domingue and Tania D. Mitchell, 55-66. Albany: State University of New York Press, 2019.

Love, Barbara J., and Valerie D. Jiggetts. "Black Women Rising: Jumping Double-Dutch with a Liberatory Consciousness

(Foreword)." In *Black Women and Social Justice Education: Legacies and Lessons*, edited by Stephanie Y. Evans, Andrea D. Domingue and Tania D. Mitchell, xi-xix. Albany: State University of New York Press, 2019.

Love, Bettina L., and Sarah Abdelaziz. "We Got a Lot to Be Mad About: A Seat at Solange's Table." In *Black Women and Social Justice Education: Legacies and Lessons*, edited by Stephanie Y. Evans, Andrea D. Domingue and Tania D. Mitchell, 165-179. Albany: State University of New York Press, 2019.

Marina, Brenda L. H. "Social Conceptions and the Angst of Mentoring Women of Diverse Backgrounds in Higher Education." In *Black Women and Social Justice Education: Legacies and Lessons*, edited by Stephanie Y. Evans, Andrea D. Domingue and Tania D. Mitchell, 245-258. Albany: State University of New York Press, 2019.

Mitchell, Tania. "Gone Missin': The Absence of Black Women's Praxis in Social Justice Theory." In *Black Women and Social Justice Education: Legacies and Lessons*, edited by Stephanie Y. Evans, Andrea D. Domingue and Tania D. Mitchell, 23-42. Albany: State University of New York Press, 2019.

Moffitt, Ursula, Linda P. Juang, and Moin Syed. "Intersectionality and Youth Identity Development Research in Europe." *Frontiers in Psychology* 11 (2020): 1-78.

Mwangi, Chrystal A. George, and Keisha L. Green. "Reflections on Moving Theory to Praxis: Dialectical Engagements of Black Women Faculty in an Urban High School Space." In *Black Women and Social Justice Education: Legacies and Lessons*, edited by Stephanie Y. Evans, Andrea D. Domingue and Tania D. Mitchell, 285-304. Albany: State University of New York Press, 2019.

Naples, Nancy A. "Pedagogical Practice and Teaching Intersectionality Intersectionally." In *Intersectional Pedagogy: Complicating Identity and Social Justice*, edited by Kim Case, 110-128. New York: Routledge, 2017.

Schoen, Seth, and Christopher Carter. "Contemplative Race Theory." In *Association for Contemplative Mind in Higher Education (ACMHE)*. Amherst, MA, 2013.

Smith, Michele D., and Maia Niguel Moore. "Black Feminist Thought: A Response to White Fragility." In *Black Women and Social Justice Education: Legacies and Lessons*, edited by Stephanie

Y. Evans, Andrea D. Domingue and Tania D. Mitchell, 75-90. Albany: State University of New York Press, 2019.

Steele, Jennifer. "Acknowledging Diversity in the Classroom." In *Learning to Teach for Social Justice*, edited by Linda Darling-Hammond, Jennifer French and Silvia Paloma García-Lopez, 18-21. New York: Teachers College Press, 2002.

Taylor, Keeanga-Yamahatta. "The Dialectic of Radical Black Feminism." In *Black Women and Social Justice Education: Legacies and Lessons*, edited by Stephanie Y. Evans, Andrea D. Domingue and Tania D. Mitchell, 319-376. Albany: State University of New York Press, 2019.

UNESCO. *Learning the Way of Peace: A Teachers' Guide to Peace Education* New Delhi, India: United Nations Educational, Scientific and Cultural Organization, 2001.

Narrative Pedagogies and Internal Family Systems in Clinical Pastoral Education

Natasha Huang

Starting with Story

Summer 2019. Fresh off of my first year of Ph.D. coursework, I enter into a 12-week intensive chaplaincy training program at a local hospital, also known as Clinical Pastoral Education (CPE for short). Over the course of this CPE unit, I spend 400 hours visiting patients on the floors and 100 hours in the classroom learning and debriefing with my educator and peers. My spiritual theme for this experience is Integration. How does all of who I am — my various professional experiences, my personal tendencies, and my theological beliefs — translate into the chaplain role? Who am I, and what do I stand for?

During Story Day, when I share for 45 minutes the most important pieces of my life, one of my peers says to me, "You are figuring out your identity." Rogers also speaks to the power of sharing our narrative in helping us recognize our identity. In my identity formation as a budding chaplain, a Ph.D.-in-progress, and as an Asian American woman in ministry, I had to integrate important narratives in my life and reflect upon how they intertwined with one another.

Spring 2020. The pandemic "arrives" on U.S. shores and society begins to shut down. I am nearly through with my second year of Ph.D. coursework and have also been conducting a six-month phase of pilot research with chaplains at the hospital where I completed my unit of CPE. This research has entailed interviews on how their spiritual learning themes — Acceptance, Slowing Down, Hope, Authenticity, Vulnerability, and Courage — impacted their personal and professional growth. In addition to these interviews, I hold intentional conversations with CPE educators on the process of using spiritual themes for learning, and these conversations give me a kind of narrative "literacy" of the ways that CPE can potentially transform the lives of chaplains.

41

In the midst of their clinical learning experiences, the chaplain interns I interviewed have explored some of their deepest places of wounding. The learning environment they have experienced in CPE, through an approach of working with spiritual themes and life stories, has given them an opportunity to surface old wounds or beliefs that have caused the most vulnerable parts of themselves to be "exiled," or hidden. Seen through the framework of Internal Family Systems, these "exiles" are "parts" of themselves that have not been given attention or expression, due to other "parts" of themselves that seek to hide and silence them, out of a desire to protect them. But in telling their stories, the healing of these exiles is beginning to take place. And in the process, these chaplains are experiencing profound contemplative encounters, creative vitality, and critical engagement leading to social empowerment.

Fall 2020. I return to the hospital for a year-long CPE residency. We are now six months into the pandemic, and I am beginning to see the most vulnerable, or "exiled" parts of myself—and of our society—surface. In my first unit of CPE, I felt a sense of inferiority and inadequacy as I encountered other individuals from Asian American backgrounds in the hospital who had chosen more lucrative medical professions and did not fully appreciate chaplaincy. Although I had experienced moments of transcendence when interacting with patients and their families in the hospital, I still wondered whether my presence on the interdisciplinary team was really that "necessary." My "protector" parts cared about how I was viewed by society. And although I provided spiritual care to those during times of grief, helplessness, and pain, I still struggled to acknowledge and honor the more vulnerable parts of myself that my "protectors" had exiled. During the pandemic, these exiles had a chance to be more fully acknowledged and healed.

In those days, so much of what we relied upon to make it feel secure—the "protector parts" of society, as it were—proved to be inadequate. Crisis meant that the most vulnerable parts of society were exposed—whether it be healthcare inequities and racial disparities, or whether it be the possibility of illness and death that each person faced. As a society, we were forced to reckon with grief and loss in a way that our Western Capitalistic culture never had to before. And in the midst of so much loss, I found a new way to hope.

Winter 2021. I am midway through CPE. We have just come through the first holiday surge of the pandemic, and I, along with the other frontline healthcare workers in the U.S., have received the vaccine. The pandemic has taken its toll. I have seen a COVID patient my age die, whom everyone though "was gonna make it." I have spoken with burnt-out nurses about the inequities in healthcare, how communities of color are impacted, and how medical staff "were trained to save lives, not to decide who lives and who dies." I have baptized a patient at the end of life, using my chaplain role to live into the Catholic allowance for emergency baptism, which my priest friend called, "making a perfect Catholic." I have visited a survivor of the virus, whose voice is gone but who wrote on a piece of paper, "Then COVID-19 got me sick." And I have held and hugged the family members of patients, in moments where all rules of safety and social distancing are overcome by the desire to comfort those in distress.

Around the Lunar New Year, I take a day trip to Santa Barbara, my first time away from the San Gabriel Valley where I live and work. I remember what life outside the hospital is like, and I am inspired to write. In a series of private blog posts, I recount the "Chaplain Chronicles," committing to memory experiences that had impacted me.

(Excerpts from) The Chaplain Chronicles

Haiku I: The ICU

> Patient unconscious
> Family cannot visit
> COVID restrictions

> I go to bedside
> To convey family's love
> Passing messages

> We are go-betweens
> Believing they can hear us
> And feel their loved ones

Haiku II: Grief

> Grief comes in cycles
> New loss brings up memories
> Of other losses

> We hear of old loss
> To help in current healing
> It's all related

Haiku III: Lament

> Laments are refrains
> What patients repeat often
> Notice when they do

> Helping one feel heard
> Is more healing than fixing
> We hear their laments.

I did not write these "Chaplain Chronicles," as they have come to be called, with any other intent than to record these experiences for my own remembrance. After they were written, they became a means for me to share snapshots of "what I did at work" for family and friends who were interested in knowing more and had time to read them. Although I had no intention of "proving" the legitimacy of my vocation, the narrative I crafted has *become* "proof" of the power of story in teaching chaplaincy.

Later, as I decided to include the Chaplain Chronicles in my dissertation research, as part of a collaborative autoethnography, the pedagogical functions behind this writing process became clearer. In applying the concepts of narrative pedagogy outlined by Frank Rogers, I have come to see how writing down my experiences helped me to learn about the ways that the story of COVID-19 intersected with my own spiritual and professional literacy and personal identity, provided me with contemplative encounters and critical reflection, and ultimately gave me the creative vitality to merge my own story with the larger narrative of social empowerment. I have applied these paradigms for narrative pedagogy to my understanding of my experiences.

Narrative Pedagogies and the Living Human Document

Stories matter. Humans know this on an instinctual level, and practical theologians include narrative pedagogies in their scholarly work. In my dissertation research, I reflected upon my experiences as a chaplain intern undergoing Clinical Pastoral Education in a hospital during the pandemic. I also interviewed my peers, with whom I had shared those training experiences. In the midst of overarching themes of fear, helplessness, death, and despair showcased by society and media, I (and my community of chaplain friends) found stories of hope and healing, meaning and learning.

Chaplains view their patients as "living human documents," to be read, interpreted, and respected as "narratively constituted" identities. Each patient encounter becomes a section in my book of "living human documents, to be cherished and shared respectfully with those who wanted to know. Chaplains also view themselves as "living human documents," to be understood in light of their personal history, social location, personality, theological orientation, and clinical experiences.

In my own chaplaincy journey, I have felt the need to write and share the stories that impacted me the most. Months later, I revisited my written reflections on these stories, only then recognizing the ways they demonstrated now narrative and pedagogy intertwine in human experience. This, to me, shows that narrative—both the living and telling of our stories—and the process of learning from narrative occurs whether or not we explicitly apply theory to it while it is occurring. It is a human tendency to remember and record (in some way, not necessarily through writing) our own experiences. The gift of having pedagogical paradigms for narrative is that educators can approach the process with intentionality and use it for various functions, functions upon which I will expound here.

Literacy and Personal Identity

The act of writing has both expressed and contributed to my sense of identity in becoming a chaplain. In writing, I narrate my chaplain identity as being central to my sense of purpose. To be myself is to be a chaplain, and chaplaincy is an expression of my truest sense of self. To simply tell my friends and family, "I love being a chaplain" is often not enough. It is the stories from experiences that communicate my passion for the work. These stories not only express my passion for my vocation, but they also serve to increase the layperson's "literacy" on what chaplaincy actually entails.

In chaplaincy, it is a common refrain that "if you didn't chart it, it didn't happen" — when referring to a patient visit. In our society, having things "in writing" somehow legitimizes it. During the worst days of the pandemic, I often found it difficult to feel that others had the capacity to hear me speak of my time at the hospital in detail, due to the emotional intensity of my experiences — not everyone is "up for" hearing difficult or graphic stories about loss and illness. Social convention often "exiles" those parts of our stories that are the saddest, angriest, or loneliest. In my work as a chaplain, I had the privilege of allowing my patients' "exiled" stories to be heard. But who would hear the parts of my experiences that had to do with such vulnerable feelings? In telling my story first through writing, I found that I could then say to my friends, "I wrote a series of blog posts about pandemic chaplaincy." This became an invitation for those who had true interest and capacity to ask me if they could read my writing. Those who took the time to do so were inducted into a kind of "literacy" about my chosen profession.

Understanding the heart of chaplaincy — beyond simply knowing what we "do" — is similar to the religious literacy that Rogers describes; there is overlap in the pedagogical functions in that both religious communities and the chaplaincy profession "profess that some stories are intrinsically transformative."[1] What differentiates a collection of anecdotes from "'canonical stories,' narratives that have paradigmatic authority for a community's sense of identity, integrity, and purpose" is the meaning we make from what happened. For chaplains, being able to make meaning from both our patients' experiences and our encounters with them contributes to our understanding of our vocation and builds upon our professional identity.

The efficacy of story "in conveying religious literacy" comes from the realization that the content of any tradition — whether it be

---

[1] Frank Rogers, Finding God in the Graffiti: Empowering Teenagers through Stories (Cleveland, OH: The Pilgrim Press, 2011), 35.

religious faith or a professional legacy—is "narratively constituted."[2] During my time in CPE, I referred to our hospital manual for guidelines and benefitted from our classroom times on forming my own best practices in chaplaincy. Yet the most transformational learning came from my presentation of patient experiences in verbatims and through discussions with my cohort. It was the stories from my clinical experiences that formed the content of chaplaincy, not the rules and regulations we followed in the hospital. Indeed, as I have come to learn, many of our professional best practices come from stories—examples of what to do or what not to do. Similarly, communal identity and meaning comes from remembering examples from experience. As Rogers writes, "people do not place their faith in a system of doctrine or a set of ethical commands; they place their faith in God, a specific God, who has acted concretely in history and is only known through the particularity of these concrete actions. The content of faith is a story."[3]

Rogers goes further to state that, not only are stories the substance of the content of religious faith (or, in my context, a vocational canon), "religious communities themselves are narratively constituted. The very glue that binds a people's collective identity is the story of their common journey toward a shared goal. In essence, communities *are* stories."[4] This could not be more true in the time of pandemic, when chaplains' sense of community was directly embodied in our shared experiences. Our shared goal was to be agents of healing in a time of great suffering. Our commitment to the journey was our commitment to one another.

Out of this came what Rogers has called "literacy—fluency with the language a community shares" by virtue of "knowing the narratives by which that particular community's core identity is constituted."[5] In recalling my stories of pandemic chaplaincy, I was speaking for myself and simultaneously offering a representation of the professional community as a whole, as filtered through my individual perception and interpretation. Other chaplains were able to read and relate to what I wrote, and laypersons gained a sense of

---

2 Rogers, Finding God in the Graffiti, 36.
3 Rogers, Finding God in the Graffiti, 36.
4 Rogers, Finding God in the Graffiti, 37.
5 Rogers, Finding God in the Graffiti, 37-8.

literacy through my descriptions. In entering into my experiences through story, they entered into the world of chaplaincy. I surmise that my readers' interest in chaplaincy came from genuine curiosity and their friendship with me, and it is in this sense that storytelling can transmit information (through a personal interaction or relationship) in ways that are more effective than simply "stating the facts." Thus, my writing served a dual function of identifying who I was and, in doing so, introducing others to a significant part of my identity.

Just as a community is narratively constituted, so too are individual identities.[6] As Rogers has observed, "narrative educators...recognize the importance and power of story in forming and transforming one's sense of personal identity...The self is a story—each of us, in essence, the central protagonist in the novel of our life."[7] In a training program that emphasized narrative—both through the practice of doing Story Day at the beginning of each unit, and also through the use of the Theme Approach throughout the unit—I had engaged in my own sense of identity through the stories I shared with my chaplain community throughout CPE. My process of writing the blog posts further solidified my sense of identity as a chaplain, in relation to the world outside of CPE. For me, that process of writing went beyond fulfilling assignments within my cohort; it was an act of remembrance that would last far beyond CPE.

The decision to include my blog posts in my dissertation speaks to Rogers' insight that "personal development is not a private enterprise. We construct identity within a story-saturated social context."[8] As I shared in previous sections, my original focus for research was on others' experiences—ethnography—filtered through my understanding of the subject through my own experiences. Making the shift to centering my own narrative—collaborative autoethnography—has integrated several aspects of my identity, from my social location to my vocation to my academic interests. In keeping with the CPE notion of humans as "living human documents," my narrative is a starting place for the study of self in several contexts—professional, academic, and personal. The

---

[6] Rogers, Finding God in the Graffiti, 56.
[7] Rogers, Finding God in the Graffiti, 56.
[8] Rogers, Finding God in the Graffiti, 59.

fact that "religious and cultural narratives transform meaning within identity-bestowing self-stories" is indeed a layered "dimension of narrative's effectiveness in shaping personal identity."[9] Interestingly, my writing about my professional experiences, which began as a deeply personal endeavor, is now given more meaning as I bring it into a more academic framework. Using narrative paradigms to interpret the writing and the process of writing imbues it with new meaning, and thus adds to the construction of my identity within a larger context— "life is experienced differently when interpreted through a wider horizon of narrative meaning."[10]

In Rogers' theoretical orientation, the last "dimension of narrative's contribution to identity formation" is that "the essence of …faith is living one's self-story within the interpretive landscape of the Christian narrative world."[11] In my context, I take this to mean that my personal experiences of chaplaincy are interpreted within the community and context of my CPE peers. This is why I began but did not end with my own narrative in my dissertation, but rather situated it within conversations with my peers. I am, because we are— my identity is meaningless within a vacuum and is formed through my relationships with others and my larger environment.

Contemplative Encounter

Many of my anecdotes depict the contemplative encounters that a chaplain is blessed with on the job—performing baptism for a dying patient, facilitating farewells for grieving family members, and being with those who have lost their ability to use their voice. In my interactions with patients and their loved ones, I was joining them in the co-creation of their stories, in the face of suffering and the mystery of why things were happening in such a way. Rogers writes about how "sacred stories and myths have the power to mediate an encounter with the numinous" and how reading sacred narratives helps us "glimpse for ourselves the divine realities to which these figures are so passionately pointing."[12] In keeping with CPE's understanding of those we encounter as "living human

---

[9] Rogers, Finding God in the Graffiti, 59.
[10] Rogers, Finding God in the Graffiti, 59.
[11] Rogers, Finding God in the Graffiti, 60.
[12] Rogers, Finding God in the Graffiti, 82-83.

documents," my patients were stories in themselves. Reading their stories, by bearing witness to their suffering, gave me a glimpse into some of the deepest divine mysteries known to humans — love, grief, death, and life. Encountering sacred stories through my patient visits were, for me, "portals to God."[13]

In the stillness that holds, surrounds, and permeates a sacred encounter, I see at play Rogers' insight that "narrative knowing is existential" — it is "distinct from and deeper than mere cognitive or intellectual reflection."[14] In my experience of performing baptism for a dying patient, I did not need to "know" from my Catholic priest friend that what I did was legitimate, in order to *know* that God's breath of life connected the patient with something sacred through the baptism. In the case of the patient who had no voice left but could write one sentence, I did not need to fully "know" her story in order to *know*, through being with her and holding her hand at the bedside, that what she had gone through in surviving COVID was unspeakable and had touched her on a soul level.

The beauty of the work of chaplains in a clinical setting is that, even as we uphold professional boundaries and sound judgment, the very nature of our work means that "the imagination is the medium through which the soul is accessed and engaged," and this is why the patient stories we encounter through our work "are so effective in fostering contemplative encounters."[15] Even though so much of our work in CPE requires a level of verbal processing — whether it is in speaking with patients and listening to their stories, or in writing verbatims and reflections — the stories that foster contemplative encounter often have a wordless dimension, a sense of knowing, through imagination, what it feels like to be another person. In the knowing of another person through what we sense and feel, we encounter the Divine as well. This is the kind of encounter for which no amount of training can prepare us.

Critical Reflection and Societal Empowerment

For me, the power of these sacred encounters prompted much critical reflection on what our society values, and whether those values matter at the end of life. In an American society that values

---

13 Rogers, Finding God in the Graffiti, 83.
14 Rogers, Finding God in the Graffiti, 84.
15 Rogers, Finding God in the Graffiti, 87.

youth and independence, what did it mean for me to accompany the dying and those dependent upon medical staff for survival? Just as "cultural narratives are a means of enculturation,"[16] narratives within the medical field tend to favor curative interventions and measurable results. Internal Family Systems speak to the ways that, out of a desire to protect the weak and vulnerable, "manager" parts tend to dominate our narratives. Rogers observes that enculturation, or socialization, "is the process by which a person absorbs a community's worldview, beliefs, values, ways of living, even language simply by virtue of participating in that community."[17] The interesting thing about a chaplain's role is that, by virtue of being within the hospital system, spiritual care becomes a part of a patient's treatment goals. At the same time, CPE helps chaplains engage in critical reflection, because the goals of spiritual care often nuance the medical community's assumptions on what "wellness" or "improvement" might look like. Chaplains have the unique privilege of holding space for those "exiled" parts of humanity's stories, that the "manager" parts have sought to diminish.

In my verbatim of the code blue, in which a patient who was my age passed away, I offered an alternative telling of the story in the context of prevailing medical culture that felt that "failing" to save the patient's life meant a defeat in the narrative. To me, the conversations I overheard with nursing staff gave me a window of how this code blue put them in touch with their own vulnerability and mortality. This was a key turning point in my own framing of the narrative of pandemic. For me, it was a breaking point that prompted critical reflection amongst medical staff. This critical reflection went beyond the immediate aftermath of the code blue, as my verbatim depicts. It spilled into conversations about the systemic injustices highlighted by the pandemic, and how nursing staff felt both called and ill-equipped to respond.

Rogers rightly points out that "cultural and religious narratives often enculturate in oppressive and destructive ways,"[18] furthering the need for critical reflection. My writing of the Chaplain Chronicles reflected a desire for critical reflection on cultural and religious narratives of what "ministry" or "healing" looks like—

---

16 Rogers, Finding God in the Graffiti, 106.
17 Rogers, Finding God in the Graffiti, 106.
18 Rogers, Finding God in the Graffiti, 109.

paradigms that were a part of my own spiritual formation and that I found to be ultimately oppressive (and even destructive). In my experience, the religious version of the medical establishment's focus on saving patients' lives manifested in prayers for healing and miracles. The sense of helplessness we encountered during pandemic was, for me, an opportunity to reframe what motivated us to do our jobs. Could we carry a sense of purpose and hope when a disproportionate amount of patients could not be saved, either through medical or religious means?

Here, I link Rogers' narrative pedagogical dimensions of critical reflection and societal empowerment. When the lived stories I encountered were so different from what society valued — stories of patients who died or whose lives would forever be altered by disease — the retelling of those stories gave me a space for "critical reflection [that was also] a means of personal empowerment and human agency."[19] I (and often the rest of the medical team) could not cure my patients, but our encounters were priceless and worth remembering simply because they were human encounters. This, to me, was the "good news" of an experience as painful and profound as pandemic — the reminder of humanity's inherent worth, by virtue of having existed on earth. This drives my values as a chaplain and has compelled me to share my own experiences with a wider audience. My contribution to the larger narrative of pandemic gives me a sense of social empowerment — I can participate in shifting the balance by highlighting more views than the dominant one.

Rogers writes that "Christian faith involves participation in the story of God's societal project"[20] and that this project of God's takes on historical, social, and participatory dimensions.[21] "God's project...is also a narrative project," one that moves humanity towards a world of liberation and inclusion.[22] Operating under this assumption, and in the context of the Narrative Pedagogies Project, "social empowerment pedagogy invites young people to claim their Christian vocation...to join forces with the sacred in the narrative project of God's social agenda." In a time when most others in the workforce stayed home to work remotely, the fact that I had the incredible privilege of coming into the hospital and being at the

---

19 Rogers, Finding God in the Graffiti, 111.
20 Rogers, Finding God in the Graffiti, 165.
21 Rogers, Finding God in the Graffiti, 166.
22 Rogers, Finding God in the Graffiti, 166.

52

bedside of patients whose loved ones could not enter imprinted in my consciousness the degree to which I could participate in God's presence on earth through my vocation.

For chaplains in CPE, Rogers' paradigm rings true in that "educational settings are narratively constructed," and narratives are thus "central in fostering social transformation."[23] Citing Paulo Freire, Rogers reminds us that education is inherently political and will encourage students to either accept or question the status quo and structures of oppression. I was fortunate in that my CPE Educator during the height of the first winter surge consistently empowered me to express my observations on structures of oppression that existed not only in the hospital, but also in society as a whole. We watched webinars that addressed issues of race and sexuality, and we were encouraged to write to these issues in our verbatims. Thus, my verbatim of the code blue was a step towards integrating the larger narrative of systemic racism and healthcare inequity into my clinical experience.

For educators who understand that "involvement in narrative activity is intrinsically transforming,"[24] facilitation of the narrative activity becomes rich soil for planting seeds of transformation. Rogers highlights the fact that "'right action' comes before 'right belief,'"[25] which fits well with the CPE learning model of action, then reflection, followed by new action. Code blues highlight this in that chaplains respond immediately to the code, having very little information on what is occurring prior to reaching the scene. Chaplains ascertain the situation through observation and, as needed, by asking medical staff. There is no "game plan" or prediction of what will be asked of the chaplain. But the right thing to do is to show up, every time. Our presence brings us directly into the narrative—and our potential for transformation.

Creative Vitality

The final paradigm that I reflect upon from Rogers' pedagogical framework is the use of narrative in accessing creative vitality. While the clinical setting of chaplaincy is not one that we typically associate with narrative art forms and creative expression, my

---

[23] Rogers, Finding God in the Graffiti, 167.
[24] Rogers, Finding God in the Graffiti, 168.
[25] Rogers, Finding God in the Graffiti, 168.

experiences in CPE—given the program's emphasis on story and storytelling—do speak to how "artistic activity connects us with the sacred spirit of life" because creativity brings humans close to the heart of God.[26] In the Internal Family Systems framework, creativity is an expression of our core Self—the part of us that knows how to lead all the parts of us, the "seat of consciousness."[27]

Working in a hospital setting that values facts and figures over narrative, I have found room for artistic activity as connecting us "with the sacred spirit of life," as something that is "intrinsically restorative."[28] Writing haikus on my blog brought to life what mattered most about my experiences. Stripping away the verbiage and the details, they summed up the spirit of all that chaplains offer. Poems, for many, "give beautiful shape to their experience,"[29] and for me, the syllabic containment of the haiku—limiting descriptions to five-and seven-syllable lines—helped me set free some of the deepest emotions of grief and loss. Indeed, "artistic activity heals the soul."[30] Telling our stories sometimes leads to perspective—to not take ourselves so seriously, to give ourselves grace for small mistakes, and to know we are not alone. In the midst of telling stories, there are laughter and tears—our bodies complete the stress cycle and our souls are given permission to heal.

Conclusion

So much of what we do as chaplains cannot be quantified. We do our best to put into words the moments we share with patients and their families. After each visit, we enter a chart note into the medical record, using clinical language to describe emotional and spiritual encounters. Each week, we produce written reflections that our educator and peers read. And each month, we detail one specific visit in a Verbatim, in order to revisit what was said, what could have been said or done better, and what we learned about our functioning as a chaplain.

---

[26] Rogers, Finding God in the Graffiti, 130, 32.
[27] Richard C. Schwartz, *Internal Family Systems Therapy* (New York: The Guilford Press, 1995), 39.
[28] Rogers, Finding God in the Graffiti, 131, 33.
[29] Rogers, Finding God in the Graffiti, 135.
[30] Rogers, Finding God in the Graffiti, 136.

For the purposes of my research, my personal and professional writing provided a thick description of the hospital environment, in that they bring readers into the emotional world of a chaplain. In reflecting on how I interacted with my environment—individual patients and staff, family members, and events like code blues, compassionate extubations, and viewings—I learned a great deal about what was important to me and why I chose this work. Thus, the power of narrative helped me integrate experiences that were both professional and personal.

In further analysis of both the content and the process of what I wrote, I have seen the theoretical underpinnings of narrative pedagogies at play. This is meaningful because, unlike written assignments in CPE that designate their purpose at the outset, retrospective analysis of what, for me, was an organic process, demonstrates the learning that is inherent to narrative engagement. Educators, ministers, and helping professionals alike have much to gain from engaging in the power of story in order to pass on a religious tradition, facilitate identity formation, mediate contemplative encounters, nurture critical consciousness, inspire social transformation, and embolden the artist within.

Doing so with an awareness that stories are layered, complex, and emotionally laden also invites the integration of Internal Family Systems in the work. For example, narrative pedagogies that have to do with religious literacy might function as "protector" parts in a group, preserving the parts of a community's tradition that seem most palatable or socially acceptable. A tradition or vocation seeking to "prove" itself to outsiders or to lengthen its legacy operates from this mentality of "putting our best foot forward." When the spiritual care department at the hospital asked for anecdotes to send to the fundraising efforts of the Foundation, I spoke of chaplains as "angels at the bedside"—passing along messages of love from loved ones who were not allowed inside the room, due to COVID visitation policies. Rather than focusing on the loss and helplessness of patients and their families, we showcased the usefulness of chaplains for connection and communication.

Narrative pedagogies that nurture critical consciousness or inspire social transformation, on the other hand, might surface emotions and stories that may have been "exiled" for some time, due to external systems and oppressive structures. My conversation with an ICU nurse about systemic injustice and how they affected our patients had just as much to do with her personal story as much as it had to do with facts and statistics. As a woman of color and the only black nurse on the ICU, she knew what it was like to see the best healthcare go to communities with more privilege. She straddled a fine line of advocating for patients, when they were overlooked by the care team, while still doing her job and "staying in her lane." As a chaplain, my own experiences with discrimination had a chance to be retold, in the safety of my CPE cohort. Some parts of the narrative were buried in previous seasons of my life, and only now the feelings tied to those vulnerable "parts" of my history felt safe enough to be heard.

Knowing that our stories are constantly being revised, reinterpreted, remembered, and reframed, communities invested in narrative pedagogies make room for creative vitality. This goes beyond artistic interests — creative vitality speaks to the co-creative power that humans have to partner with the Divine in discovering new ways of being. As "narratively constituted" individuals and communities, our engagement with story leads us to profound encounters with ourselves, with others, and with the Holy.

The use of narrative pedagogies within clinical training contexts may strike some as far from the "outcomes" of medicine. Even within the chaplaincy field, the language of "competencies" — the "outcomes" that CPE students work towards — seems skill-based rather than storied. And yet, behind each competency is a layering of clinical experiences (stories) that honed specific skills specific to spiritual care. Each verbatim is a mini-case study (a story) about a patient encounter. When a chaplain walks into a patient room, their intention is simply to be present to what is — whatever emotions are present, whatever physical conditions are the care receiver's reality, and whatever stories shape their hospital experience. By allowing those stories and emotions to be voiced, the connection between chaplain and patient facilitates spiritual "outcomes" such as decreased anxiety, increased sense of resilience, and sustained hope. Just as the patient's personal (medical, family, emotional) history informs their hospitalization experience, so does the chaplain's personal narrative shape the ways they provide spiritual care and hold the stories that their patients share. Story is inherent to pedagogy, whether we recognize it or not.

I write from the perspective of one who has been a CPE student and is now training to become a CPE educator. I am one who has experienced transformation through engaging with stories in intentional and integrative ways. I am also a chaplain in the hospital who takes seriously her role to "translate" patient stories into "relevant" data for the medical care team. What they see as anxiety or distress may likely have an emotional component, which if addressed with skill and compassion, can have direct benefits for the physical healing process. The care we provide to patients' families also has implications for how they recover and begin to grieve their losses.

Research continues to verify what storytellers have known all along—that trauma is stored in the body and can be passed down through generations, and that emotional and spiritual well-being have implications for health. Time will continue to tell of the implications of the pandemic on the many individuals that constitute our society, the ways spiritual care is needed in the aftermath of crisis and loss, and the role of narrative pedagogies in understanding and teaching from experience. The narrative of each "living human document" exists, waiting to be interpreted.

Bibliography

Rogers, Frank. Finding God in the Graffiti: Empowering Teenagers through Stories. Cleveland, OH: The Pilgrim Press, 2011.
Schwartz, Richard C. Internal Family Systems Therapy. New York: The Guilford Press, 1995.

"Everything Is An Invitation": How the Compassion Practice Invites a Transformation of Contemporary Christian Spirituality

Aizaiah G. Yong

An Invitation to Renewal

It is a disorienting moment in North American Christianity[1] which has most recently been a monocultural and eurocentric majority, yet now is experiencing rapid demographic changes and overall institutional decline.[2] All of this, even while more and more of those who were raised in those settings identify as agnostic, spiritual, deist, or multireligious.[3] This trend might be influenced by the incessant desire for meaning and purpose that is central to human experience but is complicated in the reality of the Anthropocene, where Christian institutions are acknowledged as implicated[4] into the sobering realities of climate degradation and supremacist ways of being that continue to destroy bonds of connection. Out of this crisis, Ewert Cousins has promoted the sense

---

[1] While I am attempting to speak of North American Christianity broadly and ecumenically, I acknowledge that I reflect upon this from my own positionality as an ordained pentecostal minister within a mainline Protestant denomination of North America, the Christian Church (Disciples of Christ).

[2] See "Signs of Decline & Hope Among Key Metrics of Faith," Barna, accessed November 29, 2022, https://www.barna.com/research/changing-state-of-the-church/.

[3] See Travis Mitchell, "About Three-in-Ten U.S. Adults Are Now Religiously Unaffiliated," *Pew Research Center's Religion & Public Life Project* (blog), December 14, 2021, https://www.pewresearch.org/religion/2021/12/14/about-three-in-ten-u-s-adults-are-now-religiously-unaffiliated/.

[4] See my articles with Amos Yong, "The Inequitable Silencing of Many Tongues: Political, Economic, and Racialized Dimensions of the Pandemic in the Spirit-Empowered Movement in the USA" and "Seeking Healing in an Age of Partisan Division: Reckoning with Theological Education and Resounding the Evangel for the 2020s" in *Faith and Reckoning After Trump*, ed. Miguel De La Torre (Maryknoll: Orbis Book, 2021) which broadly traces the participation of Evangelical Christian institutions in the perpetuation of societal inequities within North America.

that humanity is transitioning to a 'second axial age'[5] characterized by significant shifts in all arenas of shared life. In this context, where shall those who are disillusioned by their own religious communities find spiritual refuge and community? Where can they find trustworthy guidance[6] leading towards a life of increasing compassion, justice, and peace?[7] This is certainly an 'unprecedented' moment for those seeking to respond faithfully to their Christian commitments and ideals. It is clear a new way of being Christian (and in that way, religious) is being called for. As the twentieth century Christian and interreligious mystic, Raimon Panikkar poignantly puts it, "The crisis is profound: futuristic dreams are not enough to save those who will die in the meantime. Half-measures and substitutes will not do. Nothing short of a radical *metanoia*, a complete turning of mind, heart, and spirit, will meet today's needs."[8] Christian philosopher and theologian, Ilia Delio, understands this moment to be ripe for Jesus' evocation within the Gospels, declaring the need for new wineskins so that fresh life can emerge.[9] I understand this contemporary moment of multiple crises, to be an invitation for multiple new wineskins to be imagined and the renewal of Christian spirituality being one.

Hence, building upon Panikkar's eight priorities[10] of which contemporary spiritualities must consider for renewal, I would like to explore the Compassion Practice (CP) as one contemporary

---

[5] Ewert Cousins suggested a "Second Axial" period in *Christ of the 21st Century* (New York, NY: Continuum, 1994), 7ff.

[6] A phrase often used by Christian mystic, James Finley in his podcast series "Turning to the Mystics" and the need for spiritual seekers to identify spiritual teachers that can bear witness to spiritual vitality, social justice, and the possibility of intercultural belonging.

[7] I largely agree with the pragmatic stance of comparative philosopher and transpersonal psychologist, Jorger Ferrer, when considering how to discern spiritual experiences and practices by pragmatically evaluating their fruit. Do they produce spiritual narcissism or create persons and communities that are more inclusive, nonviolent, and engaged in actions that co-create more loving worlds? His episode can be found here: https://www.youtube.com/watch?v=htmTF4xAjZA.

[8] Taken from Panikkar's "Three Kairological Moments of Consciousness" in *Trinitarian and Cosmotheandric Vision* (Maryknoll: Orbis Books, 2019).

[9] See Dilio's essay, "New Wine needs New Wineskins" at https://christogenesis.org/new-wine-needs-new-wineskins/.

[10] See Panikkar's list of eight priorities for the new millennium in *Sacred Secularity* (Maryknoll: Orbis Books, 2022).

Christian path[11] which uniquely responds to them and facilitates the radical *metanoia* Panikkar describes. It is from this perspective, I will then suggest how CP may be one important example of a new wineskin for Christian spirituality writ large.[12] CP is dynamic in that it is sensitive to both the innermost joys and sorrows of the human experience in its depths; as well as evokes possibilities of compassionate social and planetary engagement which is now called upon more than ever (and especially the spiritual and religious crisis which I understand to be at the core of where many other crises unfold from and are entangled with).[13]

In particular, I would like to highlight five examples where I have been a firsthand witness to the impact of CP (as I have attended graduate level courses taught by Frank as well as being a retreatant in his well-known Compassion Retreat and a participant in other CP focused popular programming). Based on those examples, I will conclude by proposing and imagining other kinds of renewal within contemporary Christian spirituality and in dialogue with other religious and cultural traditions. My proposal builds upon the foundations of CP and imagines how other practices might emerge through embracing and emphasizing qualities of *authenticity, liminality, reciprocity, possibility,* and *reflexivity.* I believe these qualities might not only invite renewal within contemporary Christian spirituality but also spark possibilities for renewal within other cultural and religious spiritualities which are also needed at this time. The goal of this is not ultimately to defend the need for a 'Christian' spirituality in our time, but rather to consider how Christian spirituality (and specifically CP as one example) can

---

[11] Frank Rogers Jr. writes about the Christian origins and roots of the practice in his book, *Practicing Compassion* (Nashville, Tenn: Upper Room, 2015).

[12] Andrew Dreitcer has also discussed how the Compassion Practice is the first explicit practice within the Christian contemplative tradition to focus on cultivating compassion capacities. See "Skillful Means in Christian-Tradition Compassion Formation," *Mindfulness,* March 31, 2022, https://doi.org/10.1007/s12671-022-01877-9.

[13] See my articles, "All Mixed up: Multi/Racial Liberation and Compassion-Based Activism," *Religions* 11, no. 8 (August 6, 2020): 402, https://doi.org/10.3390/rel11080402. and "Critical Race Theory Meets Internal Family Systems: Toward a Compassion Spirituality for a Multireligious and Multiracial World," *Buddhist-Christian Studies* 40, no. 1 (2020): 439–47, https://doi.org/10.1353/bcs.2020.0024. Where I detail how I understand spirituality to be at the core of social healing and cosmic flourishing.

embrace and integrate more fully our contemporary context so that those those within Christianity (and those outside but impacted by it) can be opened to the possibilities of how we might collectively advance and deepen spiritual awareness for the sake of the world. It is my conviction that an important role in the human journey[14] is to embark upon the spiritual life consciously, cautiously, and compassionately and when we do, it can give rise to the healing and repair of suffering in the world, which establishes bonds of mutual companionship that affirm the rich diversity of Life itself.

Transformative Examples of the Compassion Practice

For anyone who is familiar with Frank Rogers Jr., many wonderful titles come to mind: professor, author, speaker, retreat leader, spiritual director, mentor, spouse, parent, friend, and many others (which this book attests to)! Yet, undeniably what has transformed my life the most in knowing Frank is the *way*[15] he chooses to live. Frank is a living embodiment of what renowned Christian mystic, Henri Nouwen, referred to as "The Wounded Healer,"[16] where one's own sufferings can become a reservoir of hope and life strength for others. Frank has shared publicly about his own experiences of trauma and the ways that his own journey through suffering led him to (along with others, Andrew Dreitcer and Mark Yaconelli) create the Compassion Practice. It is no small task to commit oneself to a path of spiritual healing that requires a life of perseverance, courage, devotion, discipline, and not to mention a great community of support from others. One does not have to look far in Frank's life to see each of these things and the world benefits from it. In honor of Frank's life and work (and his

---

[14] I am grateful for Raimon Panikkar's archetype of the monk who spells out how there is a human archetype available in the 'new monk' that centers upon simplicity, aliveness, authenticity, and communion. See *Blessed Simplicity--the Monk as Universal Archetype* (New York: Seabury Press, 1982).

[15] When I was in the midst of discerning what PhD program to choose, I felt immediately convinced to attend CST after meeting Frank, mostly because of the way he interacted with me interpersonally (both face to face and through email) through his compassionate attentiveness, gracious listening, and genuine desire to support others. I still benefit from these interactions to this day and cannot put into words how much this has meant as a young scholar of color navigating a world of white supremacy!

[16] See Henri Nouwen's book *The Wounded Healer* (New York: Image Books, 1972).

style as a story-teller), I would now like to tell stories from my own personal experiences with Frank (and CP at large as a facilitator) that can serve to demonstrate how I think CP does something new for contemporary Christian spirituality. It is my intention for this section to build the practical foundations for the more theoretical and philosophical reflections I will make in the next section.

I can remember vividly attending the first class I took with Frank and the care he extended to each of us as he laid the foundation for our learning which could only be experienced through intimate connection. This is no small feat when one considers the institution[17] which Frank was teaching at (and its bold commitment to religious and cultural pluralism). Frank led the way by modeling for us the kind of authentic, courageous and vulnerable posture which could lead to our growth. In typical Frank fashion, he filled the class with personal stories of tragedy, suffering, joy, humor, and everything in between (I mean, what else can one expect from Frank!), which helped reveal the true lesson: a capacity to accept both the beauty and fragility of the human condition. He ended the class with a call to practice meditation collectively (emphasizing it was not required to receive a passing grade in the class) as he shared gently, "when it comes to the spiritual life, everything is an invitation." It was this genuine warmth and graciousness that emanated from deep within him, that bore witness to the possibilities for all of us of experiencing it too. Frank's pedagogical style which is based in narrative[18] approaches, beckoned us to open ourselves up as well. In this moment, I saw the power of sincerity and respect for the spiritual path that allowed others to ease into what could otherwise be overwhelming or too intense. I noticed how growth could not be imposed on us from the outside but had to come from the innermost longings and yearnings of a person and was deeply contextualized based on personal, lived, and inherited cultural or intergenerational experiences. As the class progressed, Frank always paid special attention to each person's questions and concerns, creating space for

---

[17] One can read about the history of the Claremont School of Theology and how it became an institution prophetically committed intentional interreligious formation here: https://cst.edu/wp-content/uploads/2020/12/Final-Script-with-Footnotes-and-Image-Credits.pdf.

[18] This is actually biblical too, when Jesus was asked why he always taught in parables in Matthew 13:10-13, Jesus' response indicated that narratives were ways to open the door to deeper spiritual yearnings.

disagreement or adaptations to the practice that would better suit the person.

After this first class with Frank, I chose to deepen my spiritual practice using CP and attended one of the weekend retreats he facilitated and led in Oceanside, CA at the Benedictine monastery named the Prince of Peace Abbey. There he and his wife (who was the co-retreat leader), Alane Daughtery, led us through a series of practices that allowed us to become more present to our own experiences of compassion. I specifically wanted to take this retreat as an opportunity to inquire about my own experiences of racialization as a multiracial person and through the lenses of mixed critical race studies. It did not take long for me to notice how harmful experiences of racial oppression were present deep inside me. I finally found a place and practice which could begin to support my own tending to experiences of racial oppression and through this process, I began to notice small and subtle shifts in my own awareness of self, and how I might navigate racialized situations. It was through CP, I began to notice how our internal worlds connect to our external behaviors and that nothing about our experiences are fixed or static. It was here at this retreat, I learned the power of being honest and telling the truth in the spiritual journey which is really the open door to potentials of liberation and flourishing. In practicing CP with the leadership and presence of Frank as well as others who were trained in CP (helping to hold a compassionate container for sharing), I began to notice pockets of healing opening up. I observed how internalized oppression could be engaged through curiosity and connection and through these experiences– the idea that this might also be available to others who have suffered from experiences of racialization.[19] In my experience of engaging my own racialized sufferings through CP, I was able to experience the reality that everything present in our lived experiences is dynamic, interrelated, and has the potential for transformation.

This retreat provided critical groundwork for me to inquire how CP might be adapted and used in facilitations with others, specifically as it relates to social and intersectional oppression. Thankfully, I was introduced to the work of Christopher Carter and

---

[19] Some of the insights from this retreat were written in my journal and then shared as introductory autobiographical components to each chapter of my book *Multiracial Cosmotheandrism* (Orbis Books, 2023).

Seth Schoen, who created an entire anti-racist training thoroughly informed by CP. I have had the privilege of attending one of these workshops in the summer of 2021 through Beloved San Diego (an entire congregation that was formed and created based upon CP and its' trained practitioners) and was intrigued by the ways in which CP created capacities within others to remain open to difficult conversations, which in many other settings became too intense and caused participants to retract and disengage. The goal of their training was to create spaces for mixed groups to feel, listen, and learn about the effects of racism. Through using CP, the facilitators were able to help guide the group into co-creating a more resilient and collective energy that supported the group to continue to stay (relatively) grounded throughout the process. When experiences became too intense, that was named and compassionate interventions were spurred forward. One of the foundational tenets of the training was that CP is a profound and powerful collective and social resource that helps people and mixed groups remain courageously present through difficult moments. It is CP's profound emphasis on the recognition that all one's relations are key to healing and flourishing that I believe can help provide further basis for intersectional coalition building and allows for the practice to be of use to confront issues of social and structural oppression.

After these experiences, I chose to remain connected with CP and become a facilitator and partner with the Center of Engaged Compassion which has only deepened my network with other CP practitioners and allowed for creative new initiatives to unfold. I have had the privilege of teaching and facilitating elements of CP in other academic and organizational settings and continue to be impressed and amazed how many different kinds of experiences folks have with it. Through these various engagements, I have realized that CP does really create a spaciousness for a variety of spiritual experiences to come forth. While it can be done as an explicitly Christian practice for the purposes of Christ, it also can be embraced as a secular practice (with or without the recognition of any divine figure) simply focusing on moments of profound meaning or joy in a person's life. In this sense, CP is less about indoctrinating a person towards a particular belief in one religious tradition, but rather a way of participating with the vast experiences of the self and others in a posture of co-creativity. When introducing CP to others in non-religious settings, I have seen many instances where people have begun the long and deeply entrenched process of unlearning inherited social conditioning that comes from white supremacy culture which engrains into our mentality the (mis)belief of perfectionism and urgency.[20] Through CP, I have come to realize how important it is to pace oneself and to remember the process is just as important as the outcome. In one of these settings, I vividly remember taking time to share each of our own experience of the practice and what was emerging for each of us. I was immediately struck by the ways CP continued to open up transformation in a multiplicity of people, life circumstances, and social locations. Ultimately, I was enriched by the vast sense of compassion that was not contained or ruled by any one experience, group, religious tradition, or cultural understanding. It is beautiful to have a practice that does not seek conformity but embraces the rich and unique texture that fills each and every life. This opening became the foundation from which all other relations began to flow from, which only allowed for honest dialogue, critique, vulnerable sharing, and at times repair.

One of the last stories I would like to recount involves the importance of reflexivity within CP. I can remember being a student who was nervously awaiting and preparing for my PhD dissertation defense. I was exhausted, overwhelmed, and ready to be done with it. Yet, Frank (as my dissertation chair) emailed me the following words: "We would never schedule the oral if you were not ready for it and were already considered a pass. So this is just a conversation amongst colleagues celebrating and discussing your work. I hope you are ready to celebrate once it is over." His words of celebrating and savoring became an invitation for me to allow my experience of the dissertation defense to be contemplative rather than performative. It was really an invitation for me to speak from my heart after all my intellectual preparation had gone into it. I was so grateful he spoke those words to me and in other important milestones of my life, I have remembered not to gloss them over but savor them. This is an example of how CP changes the way we engage with the world from a place of fullness rather than scarcity. It is very important in CP to not only have new experiences of compassion to transform the person but to fully allow them to sink and settle in.

---

[20] Okun, *white supremacy culture.*

I tell each of these five stories as examples of how CP creates new paths of healing within the individual as well as in the collective. These testimonies also acknowledge the many fruits of Frank's scholarship but more importantly the living example from which his work flows. What is interesting to note about all of these examples is that while they took place in predominantly Christian settings, they also each show elements of how CP could be applicable for those who do not identify as Christian. This tells me that CP is a prime example of renewal within Christian spirituality that simultaneously allows for a person's Christian spirituality to deepen as well as invites others from non-Christian paths to deepen their own connection to the sacred work of compassion. It is thanks to the "yes" of Frank, being bold enough to go on his own healing path, that has in turn created ripple effects in the entire world inviting others on the path of continual transformation.

Imagining Qualities of Renewal Within Contemporary Christian Spirituality

In this final section, I would like to more concretely explore how the five examples which I have shared, become a concrete way to imagine a renewal of contemporary Christian spirituality insofar as they decenter colonial and supremacist ways of relating and knowing which have been historically centered and privileged. As a practical theologian, I want to suggest how my own lived experiences within CP might subsequently invite others who are committed to Christian spirituality to consider re-creating other historic practices in ways that are in greater solidarity with the contemporary sufferings and needs of the world. To do this, I will review 5 qualities that are apparent from each of the stories I have told and they are: *authenticity, liminality, reciprocity, possibility, and reflexivity*. I must also admit that I am not attempting to create a new synthesis or systematic approach to contemporary Christian spirituality through this list but instead offer a series of interweaving threads which may open new possibilities as to how spiritual practices can integrate contemporary realities, and in the hope that new spiritual practices may also be birthed in response to our moment.

66

Authenticity

When I reflect upon the work of CP, one of the most obvious characteristics of the practice is how it emphasizes *authenticity*. While authenticity can easily be lauded and cheapened as an individual's choice of self-expression, authenticity in CP is more about acknowledging and noticing all that is present within a person and an honesty with what the person experiences in their embodiment. Through CP, the practitioner is invited to know each aspect of the interior life through loving regard. The practice creates a posture of belonging from the onset as it is less important which aspect of the person's experience might be explored, but rather the focus becomes the way by which the person is present to it. Authenticity in this sense is about creating room within one's awareness to involve cultural reclamation, embodied wisdom, and truth-telling. All three of these qualities are especially important in a time where so many voices and wisdoms have been marginalized in the pursuit of "objectivity" due to legacies of colonial epistemological practices.[21] Authenticity within CP emphasizes that human knowings also arise from the body, including emotion, sensation, and intuition rather than solely intellectual ideas. CP insists each of these embodied learnings should be held, listened to, and appreciated, from within the interiority of the practitioner, even when they are 'non-normative' or counter to dominant culture. I see the capacity to bear loving witness to what has previously been minimized or disregarded as intentionally resisting hegemonic systems and social structures which seem to produce 'true knowledge' as that which only reflects reinscribes those who are culturally and racially privileged. CP resists silencing aspects of oneself but rather maintains an open and curious stance to become more aware with experience in its fullness.

Liminality

Another important quality that sits at the foundation of CP is *liminality*. Liminality within CP is the recognition that nothing within lived experience is fixed or static. Life rather, is constant

---

[21]Tema Okun has a long list of how white supremacy culture breeds the fallacy of pure objectivity." See, "White Supremacy Culture," *Dismantling Racism* (blog), accessed November 5, 2022,
https://www.resilientfamiliesgilroy.com/philosophy.

(re)transformation.[22] CP wholeheartedly embraces that all Life changes, transforms, and moves in creative ways, and invites the practitioner to participate within this by way of attention and engagement with interiority. Contrary to certain kinds of religious sensibilities from European philosophy that describe the divine as immutable or unchanging, CP embraces a fluidity within all of human experience and the sacred itself, which involves a continuous transformation. A radical embrace of the liminal can at times be unnerving but also liberating as it encourages an ongoing stance of receptivity to Life and a calmness to be extended when exploring that which seems unfamiliar. Liminality is not then a quality that should be imposed upon ourselves or others by will or strength but is rather is a tender opening to the dynamic participation in the flow of Life itself. Liminality in this sense also serves to offer new windows of connection and expansiveness to emerge that could not have been pre-planned or pre-determined. As Christianity goes through a serious transformation, Christian spirituality can only engage this through accepting the invitations of liminality.

Reciprocity

A third quality of CP is *reciprocity*. Reciprocity from the vantage point of CP is about the awareness of human experience as community and dialogue. No person is an individual but rather is one center of relations. For CP, the practice assists practitioners to become more aware of their own 'center' through the invitation to become aware of the PULSE of self and others. This acronym PULSE is about paying attention, understanding empathetically, loving unconditionally, sensing the sacred, and embodying new life. Becoming aware of PULSE is not something that is done in isolation but is based in dialogue within oneself in how the self is experiencing the larger world. The dynamic of reciprocity is so important because it relies upon the truth of interdependence within

---

[22] Raimon Panikkar emphasizes how life is *creatio continua,* which includes both continuity and rupture. Embracing liminality is the acceptance of this mystery and each being's role in it. See Bernarnd Nitsche's discussion of this, "Following Raimon Panikkar toward an understanding of creation as *incarnatio continua*" in Aurica Jax and Saskia Wendel, eds., *Envisioning the Cosmic Body of Christ: Embodiment, Plurality and Incarnation* (Abingdon, Oxon ; New York, NY: Routledge, 2020), 60-75.

all relationships thereby loosening (without minimizing or rejecting) the holds that social identifiers (such as race, ethnicity, gender, sexuality, or cultural religious identification) often burden shared social life. Additionally, reciprocity helps the CP practitioner to remember the connections with the larger cosmos and the earth. A renewal of Christian spirituality must involve intentional and conscious reciprocity as one important step away from the Anthropocentric spiritualities that have characterized much of contemporary Christian spiritual practices.

Possibility

A fourth quality to highlight is *possibility*. Within CP, there is the recognition of the sacred but does not presuppose how or what that looks like. CP invites the practitioner to name and know for themselves, who (or what) the sacred is as they know it. CP assumes that each practitioner experiences the sacred in unique and interconnected ways (whether this reality is personal as in a divine figure such as Jesus or impersonal as an energy field of the Spirit) and does not put any kind of restraints on how the divine ought to be experienced or engaged. CP also uses imagination[23] to encourage the practitioner to consider what life would be like if compassion was more deeply received into awareness. CP is an inherently pluralistic practice in that it encourages openness and sensitivity to various sources and experiences of Life so long as they increase the person's sense of expansive compassion in the world and do no harm to self or others. It is the pluralistic and adventurous element of CP that is especially important for a renewal of Christian spirituality as it emphasizes a generative creativity that is relevant and in touch with the felt sufferings of contemporary life. In the specific context of life now, a greater sense of the 'possible' counters any standard of monolithic thinking or hierarchies of supremacy (even of religious experience). A renewal of Christian spirituality ought also encourage an ongoing curiosity, playfulness, and hospitality to the unfolding of the Mystery rather than privileging

---

[23] New scientific studies performed by Christine D. Wilson-Mendenhall, John D. Dunne & Richard J. Davidson has shown that "simulating" or imagining a situation through contemplative practice to happen is as powerful as it actually happening. See "Visualizing Compassion: Episodic Simulation as Contemplative Practice," *Mindfulness*, March 4, 2022, https://doi.org/10.1007/s12671-022-01842-6.

ethnocentric expressions of familiarity which ultimately lead to nothing new.

Reflexivity

Finally, the fifth quality I would like to name is that of *reflexivity*. When it comes to integrating spiritual practices more deeply in our lives, reflexivity can only be possible through an intentional moment of resting or savoring or abiding in the truth or insight one just received. Reflexivity is very connected to the final step found within the practice of Lectio Divina (that of contemplating) which allows for the entire practice to be digested with the gift of space and time. Resting, savoring, or what I would call abiding, can be done through private conscious reflection, intentional embodied movement, or by sharing one's encounter with another trusted person who will honor and reflect back the sacred experience. In CP, savoring is essential. It could be understood as the movement of *sensing the sacred*, which can involve the presence of a divine figure or simply "recognizing and savoring the cosmic expanse of compassion that holds and heals all wounds."[24] The quality of reflexivity tells us that transformation involves the integration and assimilation of new experiences into our daily lives (which includes our bodily and somatic experiences, our ecological or cosmic experiences, as well as how we go about engaging our particular social, cultural, or institutional contexts). Here again, a practice that encourages abiding becomes countercultural to the norms of speed and acceleration which are characteristic of technocratic agendas. Reclaiming one's ability to rest and trust becomes a non-anxious (and yet deeply engaged) expression that subverts cycles of domination and oppression.

Ultimately, these five qualities can provide a few different avenues of imagining renewal within contemporary Christian spirituality, namely, the shift from individualistic, supremacist, and/or disembodied spiritual practices (which characterized much of the most recent history of Christianity since the Reformation) to what I would like to call "movement spiritualities." I refer to them as such because of thee primary reasons: 1) each quality that I have identified might be understood as an aspect or unique movement within the larger orientation of the second axial 'transition' which

---

[24] Quote taken from Frank's book, *Practicing Compassion*, 27.

my work is unfolding and 2) *movement* emphasizes the dynamic, non-linear, and relational dimensions of my proposal and 3) the notion of a movement is used in social justice oriented communities to demonstrate the power of the people over and against fear. Here I contend that authentic embodied spiritualities must be deeply accountable to (and threaded with) social movements occurring in public life. There is no future for spirituality if it is not concerned with the struggles of the oppressed. I would like to spend the final section exploring how I see CP as one example of a "movement spirituality" that could then invite further renewal in contemporary Christian spiritual communities.

The Compassion Practice: An Invitation to Movement Spiritualities

Now that we have reviewed various qualities from within CP and how they are connected to renewal within contemporary Christian spirituality, I would like the example of CP to further provide a foundation for a larger proposal as to how other historical Christian spiritual practices might be transformed. To do so, I would like to create a new category of Christian spirituality which I will refer to as "movement spiritualities." I will use this final section to further delineate specific dynamics that characterize a move toward "movement spiritualities": 1) an honest evaluation of the context by which the person or group is practicing in, 2) a shift from a mind dominant approach to an embodied and holistic mystical integration, 3) a sensitivity and conscious connectedness to all sentient life, and 4) an empowered engagement with social justice and collective healing. In this final section, I would like to speculate various ways in which these dynamics can offer something profound to our contemporary moment.

I begin with stressing the importance of a spirituality that does not live in a vacuum or is purely transcendent. A spirituality for today is one that must be radically honest about one's lived situation. An honesty of one's lived personal experience goes beyond the psychospiritual but also includes awareness of the social, political, economic, planetary, and other structural factors that impact one's life. In a time where truth is often relativized or universalized, or denied altogether, it is very important that a renewal in contemporary Christian spirituality re-emphasizes the truth revealed through the mystery of the incarnation which shows that we are all starting somewhere, rather than nowhere. A few practices that support this are family and ancestral practices, earth and land-based connections, critical reflection upon systemic issues of oppression, as well as other body-based healing modalities. As one can see, an honest evaluation of one's context is multi-dimensional and can happen in many ways; but must include speaking the truth that has been neglected, overlooked, or denied. What would it look like to create more spaces of interruption and disruption to the status quo rather than spiritualities becoming beholden to avoidance or minimization and/or spiritual-bypassing? It will only be in the presence of personal and collective truth where necessary steps of healing will emerge.

Another dynamic to consider in renewing contemporary practices of Christian spirituality is how a more holistic experience of one's body, culture, and artistic-creative sensibilities can be engaged. Many contemplative practices have involved observing one's thinking patterns and habits of the mind, yet less have emphasized how important our spiritual knowings comes from bodily sensation or through story, art, or song. These practices have not been privileged in the ways that silence, monasticism, and asceticism have and so many practices tend to neglect bodily experience and pleasure. How can contemporary practices recover and reclaim the celebration of the body and cultural insight without falling into self-centered hedonism? The future of Christian spiritualities can no longer afford to dismiss the unique cultural insights found across the world.

A third dynamic is connected to the second but extends to humanity's relationship with other-than-human beings. In many traditions, it has been common for humans to receive guidance and communication with the elements of the natural world, the animals, and other spiritual forces and in the age of modernity much of this has been discarded. Yet, there is a lot of wisdom and information that the other-than-human life is communicating and that we would be good to heed and integrate if we are going to co-create conditions of flourishing for the whole of life. What would it look like for our spiritual practices to reclaim aspects of sacred connection with life that is not human? How might this enlarge our sense of what it means to be human? The time is near for our spiritualities to remember how humans are too earth, and that no life can be excluded.

A fourth dynamic I would like to suggest is that of engaged and collective healing. While many practices tend to be individualized and are able to be practiced alone, how does our understanding of spirituality change and shift when we practice with others? What does it look like for our practices to be shared with others and to receive critical and constructive feedback from diverse others about them? What would it mean for us to be accountable to one another so that our behaviors and new ways of being and living, can offer healing and wholeness to the entire world? What does it mean for our communities of practice that some spaces may be closed with the recognition that not all spaces are designed for everyone? How might such particular arrangements embrace the local and subjective in new ways? While these questions could be perceived by some as exclusive, how might an ability to embrace our limitations and contingencies actually support us to be more inclusive? These are not questions that can be answered alone but only in the context of multiple communities. We are now living in an era that is ripe for more pluralistic and spiritual communities to emerge. An acceptance of that which is truly different is the courageous, vulnerable, and definitive task of our day. For it is only through relationality where equitable and liberative futures can be forged.

Conclusion

While CP is one profound invitation to re-contextualize spiritual practice in the contemporary era, I hope that its' presence will also spark larger questions into how and why we practice and what are the most needed transformations we might usher forward. Spiritual practice is also political and new expressions that are informed by social and political analysis must be integrated. Though I suspect there are many other avenues towards this harmony, I hope this reflection germinates the seeds I have received from practicing compassion with Frank. It is with profound gratitude that I wish to acknowledge the countless ways he has taught, served, and embodied the compassion he preaches. My wish is that this offering extends the legacy of Frank and might serve to broaden our sense of self, to strengthen and expand our openness to relate to others, and

73

to activate hope so that other worlds of nourishment, love, beauty, and celebration become realized. May it be so.

Bibliography

Barna. "Signs of Decline & Hope Among Key Metrics of Faith." Accessed November 29, 2022. https://www.barna.com/research/changing-state-of-the-church/.

Cousins, Ewert. *Christ of the 21st Century*. Rockport, Mass: Continuum, 1994.

Deilo, Ilia, "New Wine needs New Wineskins." Center for Christo Genesis.

June 21, 2021.https://christogenesis.org/new-wine-needs-new-wineskins/.

Dreitcer, Andrew, "Skillful Means in Christian-Tradition Compassion Formation." *Mindfulness.*

(2022).

Ferrer, Jorge, "The Future Faces of Spirit" The Integral Stage. 2020.

https://www.youtube.com/watch?v=htmTF4xAjZA.

Finley, James. "Turning to The Mystics" Apple Podcasts Preview. August 29, 2022.

https://podcasts.apple.com/us/podcast/turning-to-the-mystics-with-james-finley/id1494041647

Jones, Kenneth and Okum, Tema. *Dismantling Racism: A Workbook for Social Change Groups.*

2001.

https://www.thc.texas.gov/public/upload/preserve/museums/files/White_Supremacy_Culture.pdf.

Mitchell, Travis. "About Three-in-Ten U.S. Adults Are Now Religiously Unaffiliated." *Pew*

Research Center's Religion & Public Life Project (blog), December 14, 2021.

https://www.pewresearch.org/religion/2021/12/14/about-three-in-ten-u-s-adults-are-now-religiously-unaffiliated/.

Nitsche, Bernard. " in Jax, Aurica, and Saskia Wendel, eds. *Envisioning the Cosmic Body of*

Christ: Embodiment, Plurality and Incarnation. Abingdon, Oxon ; New York, NY:

Routledge, 2020.

Nouwen, Henri. *The Wounded Healer*. New York: Doubleday & Company, Inc., 1972.

Okun, Tema. "White Supremacy Culture." *Dismantling Racism* (blog). Accessed November 5, 2022. https://www.resilientfamiliesgilroy.com/philosophy.

Panikkar, Raimon, "Three Kairological Moments of Consciousness" *Trinitarian and*

Cosmotheandric Vision, Opera Omnia Volume VIII. Maryknoll: Orbis Books, 2019.

Rogers, Jr., Frank. *Practicing Compassion*. Nashville: Fresh Air Books, 2015.

—---. *Compassion in Practice: The Way of Jesus*. Illustrated edition. Nashville:

Upper Room Books, 2016.

Wilson-Mendenhall, Christine D., John D. Dunne, and Richard J. Davidson. "Visualizing

Compassion: Episodic Simulation as Contemplative Practice." *Mindfulness*, March 4, 2022. https://doi.org/10.1007/s12671-022-01842-6.

Yong, Aizaiah, *"Multiracial Cosmotheandrism: A Practical Theology of Multiracial*

Experiences." Maryknoll: Orbis Books, 2023.

Yong, Aizaiah. "All Mixed Up: Multi/Racial Liberation and Compassion-Based Activism."

Religions volume 11, no. 8 (2020): 402.

Yong, Aizaiah. "Critical Race Theory Meets Internal Family Systems: Toward a

Compassion Spirituality for a Multireligious and Multiracial World." Budhist-Christian Studies 40 (2020): 439-447.

Yong Amos and Yong, Aizaiah. "The Inequitable Silencing of Many Tongues: Political,

Economic, and Racialized Dimensions of the Pandemic in the Spirit-Empowered Movement in the USA Evangel for the 2020s." in Wonsuk Ma, Opoku Onyinah and Rebekah Bled, (eds). *Good News to the Poor: Spirit-Empowered Responses to Poverty*. Tulsa, OK: ORU Press, 2022.

Yong, Amos and Yong, Aizaiah. "Seeking Healing in an Age of Partisan Division: Reckoning with Theological Education and Resounding the Evangel for the 2020s." in Miguel De La Torre (ed). *Faith and Reckoning After Trump*. Maryknoll: Orbis Books, 2022.

Frank Rogers Jr. as a Practical Theologian

Sheryl Kujawa- Holbrook

Those interested in gaining an understanding of how the vocational themes of Frank Rogers Jr. interconnect are encouraged to look at his novel, *The God of Shattered Glass.*[1] Considered a "theological thriller" by one reviewer, the story is grounded in both profound trauma and abiding hope, based in a spiritual journey toward healing and transformation. As the story goes, psychologist Tony Backman is a child psychologist and narrative therapist based in a residential treatment center in northern California. Despite his "successful" practice using narrative to heal the trauma experienced by troubled young people, Tony is too tired and too depressed to deal with his own unresolved childhood issues. Until eleven-year-old Carey Foster enters his life in a locked ward and disturbs the status quo. Carey's journey toward healing from abuse is intertwined with Tony's own trauma and spiritual questions. Spiritually, the book reveals God's compassion for all, amid the divine call to practice compassion, including self-compassion, as a means of personal empowerment and social transformation.

As a graduate of the doctoral program in practical theology with an emphasis in Christian education at Princeton Theological Seminary (PTS), one of the most important centers in the development of the field, Frank Rogers' academic training was no doubt thoroughly based in the theory and history of the discipline. One of his mentors, practical theologian, and educator Craig Dykstra, redefined the concept of *practice* as a pattern of spiritual engagement that forms individuals and communities.[2] Yet, Frank is not the type of scholar to spend a lot of his time defining or defending the parameters of academic disciplines. Rather, his approach reflects the commitment of the practical theologian to interdisciplinarity and critical discernment across and beyond the

---

[1] Frank Rogers Jr. *The God of Shattered Glass.* (Eugene: Resource Publications, 2011.)
[2] Bonnie J. Miller-McLemore, "The Contributions of Practical Theology," in *The Wiley Blackwell Companion to Practical Theology,* ed. Bonnie J. Miller-McLemore (Malden: Blackwell Publishing Ltd., 2017), 2-3.

boundaries of traditional academic disciplines and methodologies. Like most practical theologians, Frank's academic interests emerge out of his social and political commitments. His passionate engagement with human, societal, and planetary healing reflect his vibrant spirituality. Though originally located within the disciplines of theology, spiritual formation, and Christian education, the generative progression of Frank Roger's work encompasses the four emphases traditionally found in the field practical theology. That is, practical theology as the *activity* of reflection on lived religion; as a *method* for doing theology; as a *curricular area* devoted to practice; and as an *academic discipline* that supports all the other areas. All four of these emphases are interconnected and interdependent and reflect the complexity of the field of practical theology today.[3]

The patterns which emerge from *The God of Shattered Glass*, reveal three major discernable themes that characterize Frank Rogers as a practical theologian. When viewed together, they represent his vocational focus and contributions to a generation of young people, theology students, spiritual directees, retreatants, social activists, workshop participants, as well as family members and colleagues. These themes are *narrative pedagogies, radical compassion*, and *healing and reconciliation*.

Narrative Pedagogies

Frank Rogers is a powerful storyteller. Anyone who has been in one of his classes, or workshops, or reads his work will see the evidence of Frank's commitment to the power of story to effect healing and reconciliation. In practical theological terms, witnessing to the suffering of another is an act of compassionate solidarity. Healing and reconciliation are interpersonal, as well as cultural and political. Through compassionate solidarity suffering is transformed and makes healing and reconciliation possible.[4]

Frank's approach to practical theology is also autobiographical, standing in the intersection of life and work. First awakened to the power of story by a youth minister in his own life, Frank's work is animated by the stories of those which inspire him

---

[3] Miller-McLemore, "The Contributions of Practical Theology," 5.
[4] For a discussion of the role of suffering in practical theology, see Pamela Cooper White, "Suffering," in *The Wiley Blackwell Companion to Practical Theology*, ed. Bonnie J. Miller-McLemore, 9-10.

and give him hope for the world. His writing often is immersed with story. One of his books opens with a story about the circle of care surrounding a family bereavement: "That circle holds blood relatives and in-laws, laughter and tears, daytime dancing and nighttime vigils, life and death. It is a sacred circle in which we glimpse God's loving presence that encircles every particle of creation."[5] The acknowledgements and introductions in his published work frequently make the connections between his academic life and lived story. "A host of people taught me that stories are not only lovable, they are liberative. I attribute to them my transformation from storyteller to narrative educator," he wrote.[6]

As a practical theologian, Frank Rogers privileges the significance of lived experience and human context; theological discourse begins and ends with practice. The use of narrative approaches has always been part of theological reflection of lived religious practices – what is now considered practical theology.[7] Practical theologians argue that theology emanates from narrative and religious community, not doctrine and "universal" experience.[8] In this way, Frank's scholarship reinforces the notion that practical theology is "bidirectional." That is, from a practical theological perspective, theology is not only tested in practice, but is inherently performative and enacted. Only secondarily is it systematized and written down. "Orthopraxis precedes Orthodoxy."[9] As one practical theologian argues, "Theology is sacramental, incarnational, and enacted. It is talking about God as embodied in faith-filled practices."[10]

In his inaugural lecture at Claremont School of Theology (CST) in 1991, "Dancing with Grace: Toward a Spirit-Centered Education," Frank developed his definitions of the purpose of

---

[5] Frank Rogers Jr., *The Way of Jesus: Compassion in Practice* (Nashville: Upper Room Books, 2016), 6.

[6] Frank Rogers Jr., *Finding God in the Graffiti: Empowering Teenagers Through Stories* (Cleveland: The Pilgrim Press, 2011), x.

[7] R. Ruard Ganzevoort, "Narrative Approaches," in *The Wiley Blackwell Companion to Practical Theology,* ed. Bonnie J. Miller-McLemore, 214, 218.

[8] Miller-McLemore, "The Contribution of Practical Theology," 3.

[9] Quoted from the syllabus, "Pedagogies for Justice and Conflict Transformation," by Ellen Marshall and Frank Rogers Jr., Spring 2008.

[10] Elaine Graham, "On becoming a practical theologian: Past, present and future tenses," *Theological Studies* (August 31, 2017): 5. Accessed May 4, 2022.

Christian education and the vocation of teaching based on Karl Barth's insights regarding the activity of the Holy Spirit. "The Holy Spirit is the very activity of God which awakens, frees and empowers humanity for reconciled life, a life that is lived in the Spirit," he writes. "In its deepest sense, it is the Spirit who is the Teacher. The Holy Spirit, then, is not the illuminating endpoint of the education process. She is the very context which grounds the entire educational enterprise, the very power on which education depends."[11] He then goes on to construct narrative using the metaphor of "the dance" to illustrate the work of his academic field and vocation as teacher. As do other religious educators who consider themselves practical theologians, the focus here is more concerned with the deep questions of human existence than with traditional religious instruction. Religious education that makes space to wrestle with generative narratives expands the moral imagination.[12] Frank argues that at its essence, education is not primarily tradition-centered, or Bible-centered, learner-centered, experience-centered, socially-centered, or even church-centered, but "Spirit-centered." "Its fundamental purpose is to deepen persons' capacities to see and to be taken by the reconciling activity of God in our world and in our lives and to empower persons' capacities to participate in that activity with an increasingly fluidity."[13]

As a narrative educator, Frank Rogers envisions and shapes his vocation as a teacher through guiding metaphors. He asserts that teaching is an art and a form of empowerment. He extends the metaphor of the dance to the role of teacher as the "choreographer." Through the art of teaching, our choreography, we find our faith and gain hope in a broken world. "It may be that the teaching which most fluidly mediates an increased participation in the reconciling activity of the Spirit, the teaching which is the most truly Spirit-centered, is one which arises out of and feeds back into the life of a community which faithfully gathers before the Presence which holds it, empowers one another in fullness of life and moves

---

[11] Frank Rogers Jr., "Dancing with Grace: Toward a Spirit-Centered Education," *Occasional Paper, School of Theology at Claremont* 1, no. 2 (April 1991): 1-2. At this point CST defined the field as "Christian Education," not "Religious Education" as currently stated.
[12] Carol Lakey Hess, "Religious Education," in *The Wiley Blackwell Companion to Practical Theology*, ed. Bonnie J. Miller-McLemore, 299, 307.
[13] Rogers, "Dancing with Grace," 5.

outward into the world in redemptive action; a community of which the teacher is a participant."[14]

Throughout Frank Rogers' scholarship and teaching he demonstrates the power of story to heal and to enact social change. "To be sure, God can be known in the intrinsically valuable process of youth telling their own story and claiming artistic freedom to express that story honestly and truthfully," he writes. "In creating mirrors of teen experience in their community, they invite others to see their world and to emphasize with the stories that compose their lives."[15] Frank's work is not about reducing practical theology to autobiography. Rather, he uses story as a critical lens for reflection on human experience and divine encounter in context. The use of narrative approaches as a tool for healing African Americans, women, and other marginalized peoples is advocated by practical theologians and clinicians like Edward P. Wimberley and Christine Cozad Neuger. The use of narrative facilitates engagement with "the fullness of personal, communal, spiritual, and political dimensions of human stories."[16]

In 2002, Frank established the Narrative Pedagogy Project at CST with a mandate to explore the role of the narrative arts (storytelling, creative writing, drama, autobiography, etc.), in nurturing theological reflection, spiritual vitality, and social empowerment among young people. Although the target audience at the time were teenagers, the deep learning and the model of the project became an integral part of the CST curriculum. Narrative pedagogies are a distinctive component of the curriculum as well as a favored research methodology among doctoral students. CST students grounded in narrative theoretically, observe live groups, and practice with supervision. Narrative pedagogies as a tool for healing and reconciliation birthed CST-based projects as diverse as religious tolerance in Pakistan, social empowerment of Korean women, abuse recovery for young people, affirming African American cultural identities in neighborhoods vulnerable to gang

---

[14] Rogers, "Dancing with Grace," 8.
[15] Rogers, *Finding God in the Graffiti,* 506.
[16] Mary Clark Moschella and Lee H. Butler, Jr., eds. *The Edward Wimberley Reader. A Black Pastoral Theology* (Waco: Baylor University Press, 2020), 76.

violence, and AIDs education in Zimbabwe.[17] Although the diverse participants involved encountered God using narrative, they experienced the sacred in divergent ways. "In short, the field of narrative pedagogy is analytically entangled, a graffitied wall, if you will, where different narrative understandings, like spray-painted monikers and fluorescent taglines, are jumbled over, though, and within one another often in the same educational program."[18]

As a spiritual practice, the essence of narrative pedagogies is to empower people to narrate their lives with meaning and purpose. Through his study of narrative pedagogies, Frank identified six distinctive types. The first, narratives focused on *religious literacy*, teach the essential stories of a faith community. *Identity formation* is the focus of the second type of narrative pedagogy that supports people in constructing their life stories. The third type of narrative pedagogy, *contemplative encounter*, cultivates and mediates the presence of God. *Critical reflection* is the fourth type of critical pedagogy that awakens critical consciousness. The fifth type of narrative pedagogy, *creative vitality*, recognizes the healing and transformative impact of artistic expression. Lastly, *social empowerment*, the sixth form of narrative pedagogy, empowers collective agency. All six forms of narrative pedagogies offer opportunities for mediating the sacred and envisioning a more just and peaceful world.[19]

The use of narrative pedagogies is also a critical methodology for practical theologians concerned with embodied religious belief and the sacred revealed in the daily lives of individuals and communities. Stories not only reveal the present experience of the sacred for individuals and communities but envision ways we might live more fully into the future. It should also be noted here that the practices of narrative pedagogies that foster deep dialogue also generate the deep connectedness necessary to build genuine pluralism. In this way, narrative pedagogies support dialogue across divisions, such as in interreligious engagement and racial

---

[17] Frank Rogers, Elizabeth Conde-Frazier, Andy Dreitcer, "Project on Cultivating Youth for Christian Leadership Using Narrative Pedagogies," Proposal Narrative. Claremont School of Theology, August 2006.

[18] Rogers, *Finding God in the Graffiti*, 16-17.

[19] Rogers, *Finding God in the Graffiti*. The overview of the six types of narratives pedagogies is found on pages 17-19; each chapter of the book focuses on one of the types in detail.

justice initiatives, by reclaiming voices from the margins, and focusing the theological task on a shared commitment to practices, rather than on white-male-Christian-dominated-hierarchies. Certainly, within the context of CST, the narrative pedagogies tradition of the curriculum contributes to a climate of reflexivity and dialogue that has supports an ever-changing and increasingly diverse student body, many of whom are doctoral students in practical theology.

Radical Compassion

Practical theology has a deep commitment to compassion not only as a theological construct, but as a habitus inculcating compassion for the self, for others, and for the communities in which we live. Within the context of practical theology, compassion goes beyond an individual feeling or activity. Rather, it is a dynamic process which leads to compassionate solidarity, entering the suffering of oneself and others, and making a commitment to overcoming the cause of that suffering. "The nature of the Christian life as a compassionate protest of suffering and the alignment with those who are experiencing distress and pain calls for a renewed emphasis on entering the liminal places of deepest concern and staying tethered to a compassionate engagement without fear."[20]

Frank Rogers Jr. established the Center for Engaged Compassion at CST in the summer of 2010 with faculty colleague Andrew Dreitcer to further the work of contemplatively based social compassion within the school's curriculum and beyond, through retreats, workshops, and research. Though grounded in the Jewish and Christian traditions, the work explores compassion in other religious traditions, such as Buddhism, yet is inclusive to those of no tradition. What became known as the Compassion Practice was developed by Frank, Andy, Mark Yaconelli, and others and refined through the Triprykos School of Compassion at the Center for Engaged Compassion. Since there hundreds, perhaps thousands of students, retreatants, social activists, spiritual directors, and others, have participated in compassion formation classes, retreats, and workshops focused on personal healing and social transformation.

---

[20] Phil C. Zylla, "Inhabiting compassion: A pastoral theological paradigm," *Theological Studies* (31 August 2017): 8. Accessed May 12, 2022.

"Compassion is the heartbeat of humanity," writes Frank in *The Way of Radical Compassion*. "For compassion not only restores the heart of our own humanity; its healing care makes humanity once more the heart of another grown hard and cold."[21] Of course, his invitation to the way of radical compassion begins with a story about how an act of compassion from a neighbor changed the life of an inner-city boy who destroyed the man's garden. The way of radical compassion invites us to recover and retain that which is best in our humanity despite the suffering and violence in the world around us.

Frank Rogers Jr. explains the way of radical compassion as a three-fold path. *"First, the path invites us to know, in the depths of our souls, a compassion that holds and heals us."*[22] Here the invitation is to open our hearts to the sources of compassion all around us, and to be moved to the joys and sufferings of another. The world is a porous place if we choose to connect with the infinite love present in all creation. Such love has the capacity to heal the deepest wounds and invites us to be healed and held in love.[23]

"Second, the path of compassion invites us to be liberated from the internal turbulence that disconnects us from our compassionate core."[24] This second stage of the three-fold path of radical compassion is focused on self-compassion as a means towards freedom and restoration. This stage addresses the difficulty for many to experience self-love, instead succumbing more easily to inner voices that claim we are unlovable. Although the Golden Rule invites us to love our neighbors as ourselves -- meaning the care that we give to ourselves should reflect that which we extend to others – many people fall short of this invitation. Frank invites us to consider that, "Self-compassion brings us home to ourselves."[25] Self-compassion invites us to experience ourselves as beloved, and to relate compassionately to those parts of ourselves we have deemed shameful and unlovable. It is through self-compassion that we are truly able to have compassion for another, and to love our neighbors as ourselves.

---

[21] Frank Rogers Jr., *Practicing Compassion* (Nashville, TN: The Upper Room, 2015), 9.

[22] Rogers, *Practicing Compassion*, 12.

[23] Rogers, *Practicing Compassion*, 13.

[24] Ibid.

[25] Ibid.

The last stage on the three-fold path of radical compassion invites us into care for others that recognizes the inherent dignity and worth of all beings. *"Third, the path of compassion invites us to extend genuine care towards others."*[26]   Such compassion certainly extends to those closest to us, including family, friends, co-workers. But radical compassion also extends further, to include our opponents, our adversaries, our enemies. The third path of compassion refuses to demonizes the other, even those who have committed heinous crimes, leaving open the possibility of making amends and being restored to the community. It is understood that vulnerable people need protection, and that offenders need to be held accountable for their actions. Meeting adversaries with restorative care means that we retain our humanity in the face of the inhumane. "Compassion is the means to becoming most deeply human," writes Frank Rogers. "It revives the pulse of one depleted by heartbreak and suffering. It sustains the pulse of interior freedom and grounded empowered care. And it resuscitates the pulse of the person deadened by brutality, uniting him or her once more with the human community."[27]

The Compassion Practice is Frank Rogers' response to the question of *how* to cultivate the compassion that we and the world so deeply need to restore the heartbeat of our humanity. Therein lies the difference between intellectual assent to the idea of a more compassionate world and inhabiting it and cultivating it. To be sure, practicing compassion is challenging; practices take *practice* to become part of daily life and how we experience the world. On the surface, however, the Compassion Practice is relatively simple: 1) *Catch your breath* (Get grounded); 2) *Take your PULSE* (Cultivate compassion for yourself); 3) *Take the Other's PULSE* (Cultivate compassion for another); 4) *Decide what to do* (Discern compassionate action). In the Compassion Practice "PULSE" refers to "taking our own pulse," or a recalibration, a turning inward, that gets us back in touch with the heartbeat of humanity.[28] The acronym for the PULSE of compassion stands for *Paying attention* (Contemplative awareness); *Understanding emphatically* (Empathetic care); *Loving with connection* (All-accepting presence); *Sensing the sacredness*

---

[26] Rogers, *Practicing Compassion*, 14.

[27] Rogers, *Practicing Compassion*, 14-15.

[28] Rogers, *Practicing Compassion*, 19, 29-31.

(Spiritual expansiveness) and *embodying new life* (Desire for flourishing). From the PULSE springs compassionate action towards others and the world. [29]

In Frank Rogers' work the power of the Compassion Practice is inextricably linked to compassionate action. The spiritual roots of compassionate actions affirms that genuine compassion is *engaged* compassion. True compassion is embodied and involens a tangible response. The embodiment of compassion takes many forms; generosity, service, witness, solidarity, empowerment, and justice, to name several. At times the compassionate response to a situation is evident; at other times the compassionate response requires discernment. "Compassion intends to ease suffering and promote the flourishing of life," writes Frank Rogers.[30] Genuine compassion springs forth from abundance and promotes flourishing and restoration in ourselves and others. Those actions that do not embody compassion "diminish our humanity, minimize our needs for healing and wholeness, leave us vulnerable to violation, silence us, eclipse us, or render us powerless."[31]

One of the distinctive contributions of Frank Rogers' work on the way of radical compassion is his inclusion of the Christian tradition as part of the conversation. His writing on Jesus' spiritual path provides insights on the deep roots of the compassion tradition which are often eclipsed by institutional Christianity or focus on compassion from the perspective of other religious traditions. In practical theological terms, spirituality is concerned with the embodiment of a way of life, the teaching of spiritual wisdom, and critical reflection on traditions from the perspective of justice.[32] Frank's work in radical compassion is built on the assumption that the tradition of embodied compassion was the way of the followers of Jesus of Nazareth from its inception. Admittedly, Jesus of Nazareth was not a Christian, nor did he set out to start a new religion. This said, Jesus was a spiritual teacher who embodied the compassionate love of God. Frank Rogers, as a narrative educator, notes that it was not only Jesus' message that was radical, but it was *the way* in which he taught it. "It offered a radical understanding of

---

[29] Rogers, *Practicing Compassion*, 22-27.
[30] Rogers, *Practicing Compassion*, 110-115.
[31] Rogers, *Practicing Compassion*, 115-116.
[32] Claire E. Wolfteich, "Spirituality," in *The Wiley Blackwell Companion to Practical Theology*, ed. Bonnie J. M Miller-McLemore, 2017), 334-335.

an extravagantly loving God and how such a God could be known; it promoted a radical sense of human dignity and a capacity for emboldened and abundant life; and it cultivated an ethic of radical care that extended not only to loved ones, neighbors, and strangers but also to enemies, opponents, and oppressors."[33]

Frank argues that the essence of Jesus' spiritual path is the cultivation of compassion. The God that Jesus knew so intimately and who inspired his ministry was the divine source of all life. Jesus' emphasis on love was intended to inspire his followers to embody this love through compassionate action in the world. "As he teaches in the parable of the final judgement where the sheep and the goats are separated, the extent to which we embody love can see through the following litmus test: Do we feed the hungry, satisfy the thirsty, welcome the stranger, clothe the naked, free the oppressed, and visit the sick and imprisoned?"[34]

This emphasis on the need for concrete embodiment to practice true compassion and effect healing and reconciliation is a key component of how Frank Rogers' work relates to practical theology. At its essence, practical theology is about the embodiment of religious beliefs in lives of individuals and communities. We know from personal experience and from interdisciplinary research that authentic healing is organic much like trauma is organic, and connected to our whole psychological, spiritual, and physical selves, as individuals and as communities. In practical theological terms, these connections are illustrative of the dialogical relationship between theory (from a range of disciplines including but not limited to scripture and theology) and practice, that is integral to the way we approach all theological questions.[35] Embedded in this commitment to embodiment is the belief that spiritual formation is based in relationship; we are invited into relationship with the Holy One on all levels of our being. This invitation does not negate the importance of intellectual theological discourse, rather it is an opportunity to incorporate our whole selves into the relationship with the ultimate vision of divine flourishing for all creation. We

---

[33] Frank Rogers, *The Way of Jesus,* 13.

[34] Frank Rogers, *The Way of Jesus.* 116.

[35] For example, one scholar describes the development of practical theology as an academic discipline in the following: Chang Kyoo Lee, "Practical Theology as a Theological Discipline," *Korean Journal of Christian Studies* 75 (March 2011): 315. Accessed May 1, 2022.

engage the sacred as embodied beings, not when reduced to disembodied brains.

Healing and Reconciliation

The necessity of embodied practice leads to the third emphasis in Frank Rogers work, healing and reconciliation. In "Dancing with Grace," Frank writes that the dance is not limited to a single learning environment but moves through creation toward the kin-dom of God in the world. "The dance of the reconciling Spirit does not remain closed, rather it moves through the suffering, the oppression, the pain and the injustice of the world. The dance, to be sure, is not triumphalist in these places; it is a dance of mourning, of outrage, of yearning. Yet it is still a dance, still free movement; it is a dance of hope nurturing peace, healing, and justice."[36]

Within Frank Rogers' vision of religious education, and by extension practical theology, the teacher recognizes their role in the dance of healing and reconciliation and is sensitive to the call of the Spirit at work in broken places. "If teaching is to give rise to a movement outward toward the Reign of God, then the teaching environment itself should be a whisper of that Reign and a space where strangers are welcomed, the voiceless are given speech, and painful issues and questions are endured."[37]

Renown religious educator, scholar, pastor, and author Elizabeth Conde-Frazier worked with Frank at CST and was a collaborator on the Narrative Pedagogy Project. She comments on his commitment to healing and reconciliation: "Frank was not only a brilliant teacher and scholar who could put together information in logical and summarized fashion, but he was a healer who made sure that the empowerment of persons at different levels was his commitment as an educator. Frank understood that it is from our wounds that many times flow our passions and so he was not afraid to lean into his own wounds and to help others, through spiritual practices, to do the same. Leading persons into spiritual practices that would heal and empower is not an easy task especially as he facilitated and taught us to embrace the spiritual diversity represented in the midst of the participants. He taught persons to

---

[36] Rogers, "Dancing with Grace," 7.
[37] Rogers, "Dancing with Grace," 7-8.

become courageous because he facilitated that way to tap into one's spiritual resources for doing so."[38]

The emphases of narrative pedagogies and radical compassion connect with Frank's life-long commitment to social justice and peace-making practices. In a book project edited by former CST colleague and social ethicist Ellen Ott Marshall, Frank contributed an article entitled, "Loving our Enemies: Contributions of the Narrative arts to a Practice of Peacemaking."[39] Here Frank engages with a variety of narrative pedagogies – storytelling, playmaking, stage drama, and creative writing – to stimulate the moral imagination, envision compassionate action, gain insights about faith, and practice peacemaking skills. Beginning with Jesus' invitation to nonviolence, and the work of Walter Wink, the chapter explores the challenging and counter-intuitive command to love our enemies. "Jesus' nonviolent invitation is an empowered form of action that refuses to be humiliated, claims one's dignity in the face of dehumanization, seizes the initiative, and invites the aggressor into an appropriate mutual relationship," he writes. "Such action may be dangerous – a master may beat the insolence out of a slave turning the cheek, a motorcyclist may blow up in rage. But the action is not a cowering acquiescence to an oppressive situation. Turning the other cheek is standing up for dignity." [40]

Through a series of stories, the chapter goes on to illustrate the practice of restorative justice as the path of healing and redemption and explores the nuances between accountability and vengeance. Importantly, the spiritual gift of our enemies resides in their embodiment of our collective shadows, those parts of ourselves that we deny and dread. "The spiritual gift of our enemies is that they reveal that evil which still resides in our own souls. With the clarity of a freshly polished mirror, they expose the violent impulses, the deep-seated wounds, or the unsatisfied yearnings that lie within ourselves."[41] The invitation to peacemaking requires us to hold ourselves and others in compassion until the woundedness is

---

[38] Elizabeth Conde-Frazier, email to author, June 7, 2022.
[39] See Ellen Ott Marshall, *Choosing Peace Through Daily Practices* (Cleveland: Pilgrim Press, 2005).
[40] Frank Rogers Jr., "Loving our Enemies: Contributions of the Narrative Arts to a Practice of Peacemaking," published in Marshall, *Choosing Peace Through Daily Practices*. Manuscript edition, 5.
[41] Rogers, "Loving our Enemies," 19.

transformed by the Spirit and healed. The compassionate action of peacemaking requires that we hold with compassion the enemies around us, as well as those within us. The process of peacemaking is both messy and complex. "Loving our enemies is an agonizingly challenging practice of Christian peacemaking."[42]

The study of peace education within the framework of spiritual formation, religious education, and ethical reflections is one of the many contributions Frank Rogers brings to the CST curriculum. A course he co-taught in 2008 with Ellen Ott Marshall, "Pedagogies for Justice and Conflict Transformation," illustrates Frank's commitment to ensuring that students entering the ministry or destined to become academics are well-schooled in the assumption that "Orthopraxis Precedes Orthodoxy."[43] Such education requires that not only the course materials, but the process of the class reflects the values of peace with justice. Through their collective experience, the class discerns the open wounds in their community and the world, and together reflect on and develop faithful and transformative responses. This illustration of one of Frank's collaborative courses is but one example of his commitment to healing and reconciliation in all his classroom activities.

As Elizabeth Conde-Frazier reflects: "Social justice was also a commitment in his teaching. He understood it was a goal for one's work as a religious educator. To do all these things, Frank arranged and rearranged classrooms, was willing to work with partners in his classrooms and was confident in ushering in the nontraditional. This is what drew students to him, especially students who wished to understand transformation. Narratives became an important part of this. Frank certainly led by example. We all understood that religious education began with authenticity, with being ourselves."[44]

By being himself, Frank Rogers Jr. has made an indelible contribution to the endeavor of practical theology at Claremont School of Theology and beyond. His own work, as well as that of the

---

42 Rogers, "Loving our Enemies," 23.
43 Ellen Ott Marshall and Frank Rogers Jr, "Pedagogies for Justice and Conflict Transformation," Couse syllabus, Spring 2008.
44 Elizabeth Conde-Frazier, email to author, June 7, 2022.

hundreds of students around the world he mentored over the years, embody the values of narrative pedagogies, radical compassion, and healing and reconciliation into their lives and vocations. A teacher could ask for no deeper legacy.

Bibliography

Graham, Elaine. "On becoming a practical theologian: Past, present and future tenses,"
Theological Studies, August 31, 2017, 5. Accessed May 4, 2022.

Lee, Chang Kyoo, "Practical Theology as a Theological Discipline," *Korean Journal of*
Christian Studies 75, March 2011, 293-320. Accessed May 1, 2022.

Rogers, Frank Jr., "Dancing with Grace: Toward a Spirit-Centered Education," *Occasional*
Paper, School of Theology at Claremont 1, no. 2, April 1991.

Rogers, Frank Jr. *Finding God in the Graffiti.* Cleveland: The Pilgrim Press, 2011.

Rogers, Frank Jr. *The God of Shattered Glass.* Eugene: Resource Publications, 2011.

Rogers, Frank Jr. *Practicing Compassion.* Nashville: The Upper Room, 2015.

Rogers, Frank Jr. *The Way of Jesus: Compassion in Practice.* Nashville: The Upper Room, 2016.

Marshall, Ellen Ott. *Choosing Peace Through Daily Practices.* Cleveland: Pilgrim Press, 2005.

Miller-McLemore, Bonnie J., ed. *The Wiley Blackwell Companion to Practical Theology.*
Malden: Blackwell Publishing, Ltd., 2014.

Moschella, Mary Clark and Lee H. Butler, Jr., eds. *The Edward Wimberley Reader. A Black Pastoral Theology.* Waco, TX: Baylor University Press, 2020.

Zylla, Phil C. "Inhabiting compassion: A pastoral theological paradigm," *Theological Studies,* 31 August 2017, 8. Accessed May 12, 2022.

Peregrinatio: Sacred Wandering for Christ and the Power of Compassion

Joung Hee Kim

Peregrinatio or sacred wandering is one of the representative spiritual practices of Celtic spirituality. Still today, it can offer Christians insights and be a helpful spiritual practice, especially for those who identify themselves as exiles, immigrants, or wanderers. For *peregrinatio* can give us a spiritual framework for seeing ourselves as pilgrims of Christ, as seeking God's will. In such sacred wanderings, *peregrini*[1] journeyed to seek God's will, and tried to be led by the Holy Spirit rather than setting a particular destination. To follow the path of Jesus Christ, who himself lived on earth as an exile, *peregrini* through the ages have left their homes, possessions, families, and friends to become exiles. While they engaged in *peregrinatio*, they either stayed in their homelands or journeyed to others, according to God's will. Such journeys as foreigners involve both outward and inward wanderings. For even when their pilgrimages and roamings take *peregrini* to foreign, strange, and barren lands, such wanderings also entail their inward journey. For pilgrims leave behind—for a while or forever—their attachments, whatever hinders their encounter with their true selves and with the presence of God. In this inward journey, *peregrini* continuously contemplate their existence and God. The spirituality of *peregrinatio* invites them—and us—to be present in the moment and to become more loving persons in our sacred wanderings on earth.

While the original version of *peregrinatio* required a lifelong commitment and considerable risk, we can appropriately integrate this practice into our daily twenty-first-century lives according to our convenience and to whatever degree suits us. In particular, we can integrate peregrination in our daily walking contemplative practice and compassion practice. The compassion practice of the Center for Engaged Compassion, developed by a co-director of the center and a professor at Claremont School of Theology Frank

---

[1] Plural of *peregrīnus,* a person who engages in *peregrinatio.*

Rogers Jr., well expresses the process and spirituality of *peregrinatio* and it can be one of the effective modern applications of *peregrinatio*.

In this article, I first explore the historical background and development of *peregrinatio*, its essential movements, purposes, and outcomes to establish its contours. I subsequently enumerate the practice's insights and wisdom, as well as its applications for Christian who identify themselves as wanderers.

Historical Background and Development of Peregrinatio[2]

Celtic people are generally understood as those who came from the Mediterranean region to the British Isles. This implies that they were originally immigrants. Christianity was introduced to the Celts around the fourth century. Having strong communal values, Celts embraced the monastic tradition, and in countries in which Celts settled, monasteries became the main institutional form of Christianity. Many Christians were attracted to desert monasticism, and story-telling about heroic holy persons was prevalent in those early centuries of the Church. John Cassian was one such person, and he himself had been inspired by the Desert Fathers in Egypt.[3] Usually, Celtic monks worked in monasteries or engaged in "solitary contemplation in a hermit's cell."[4] But many monks also wandered from place to place as missionaries or pilgrims.[5] "The Irish church became a brilliant center of Christian culture and monastic spirituality,"[6] notes Gordon Mursell. Irish monasticism was depicted as "ascetic and educated, and [its monks] often sought exile abroad in the life of a pilgrim, in search of the kingdom of heaven"[7] — sometimes in the form of the desert. During their travels, they spread Christianity throughout the European region. "The search for the 'desert' led them to colonize with hermitages many isolated hills, islands, and headlands," as the life of famous Saint

---

[2] This and the immediately following paragraphs are part of the second chapter of my Ph.D. dissertation, entitled "Walking Contemplative Practice: Its Christian Origins, Neuroscientific Analysis, and Integration with Compassion Practice" (Ph.D. diss., Claremont School of Theology, 2022).

[3] Nora Kershaw Chadwick, *The Celts* (London: Penguin Books, 1991), 189.

[4] Ian Bradley, *The Celtic Way* (London: Darton, Longman and Todd, 1993), 71.

[5] Bradley, *The Celtic Way*, 71.

[6] Gordon Mursell, *The Story of Christian Spirituality: Two Thousand Years, from East to West* (Minneapolis, MN: Fortress Press, 2001), 77.

[7] Mursell, *The Story of Christian Spirituality*, 77.

Brigid shows.[8] Monks of the Irish monasteries were sent to pagan lands, especially the British Isles and the European Continent, in groups of two or three in order to establish "colonies of heaven,"[9] as Columba called them.

Along with spreading the Gospel, the Celts expressed their spirituality as engagement with God in their physical journeys. That physical interaction with God was important for them and often involved ascetic disciplines common at that time. Celtic spirituality is based on such disciplines, particularly on the concept of participating in the life of martyrdom. Esther de Waal identifies three forms of such martyrdom in *The Celtic Way of Prayer*, "the red, the white, and the blue or green."[10] According to De Waal, the red refers to "being killed for the faith," the white represents "renunciation of the world, the way of exile, or *peregrinatio*," in which a few chosen ones engage, and the blue or green involves "devotion to austerities," in which anyone can engage to serve God more fully.[11] Since white martyrdom refers to offering oneself to God by leaving one's place and making one's journey to seek the kingdom of heaven, *peregrinatio* is classified as white martyrdom. Those who undertook this discipline desired to be exiles and pilgrims, following in the tradition of Jesus' call to his first disciples to leave their homes and families behind and follow him, an exile on earth, one who wandered from place to place without settling anywhere permanently. Bradley emphasizes that Celtic pilgrims often "sought out the most desolate, isolated, barren places"[12] instead of places of abundance.

This *peregrinatio* is not an action in which one simply wanders around somewhere, but instead is the lifelong commitment of giving oneself away for God. According to De Waal, while *peregrini* aim to become "stranger[s] and [exiles] to all that is familiar [and] safe," they take Christ as an example who willingly came on the earth.[13] Thus, engaging in *peregrinatio* can be the means to imitate Jesus' "voluntary exile."[14] For the *peregrini*, this voluntary

---

[8] Mursell, *The Story of Christian Spirituality*, 78.
[9] Bradley, *The Celtic Way*, 74.
[10] Esther de Waal, *The Celtic Way of Prayer* (New York: Doubleday, 1997), 132.
[11] de Waal, *The Celtic Way of Prayer*, 132.
[12] Bradley, *The Celtic Way*, 78.
[13] de Waal, *The Celtic Way of Prayer*, 4.
[14] de Waal, *The Celtic Way of Prayer*, 4.

wandering typically has no order or rules. They simply open themselves to wherever the Spirit leads them. Through this outward journey, wanderers encounter their resurrected, true selves in God. Although *peregrinatio* is an outward journey, it also has an inward aspect—both a motivation and a practice—in that it "is undertaken for the love of God, or for the love of Christ."[15] De Waal notes that as long as we undertake our journey—whatever its form—for the love of God, "Christ must already hold a place in our lives."[16] Perhaps, *peregrini* sought to be aware of the presence of Christ in them during their journeys.

Esther de Waal describes what the early *peregrinatio* looked like and how this journey was practiced. In *The Celtic Way of Prayer*, de Waal begins her introduction by comparing the journeying of Celtic spirituality with the fact that "the whole idea of the journey is basic to humanity."[17] Esther de Waal explains *peregrinatio* by telling the story of three ninth-century Irishmen who drifted for seven days in a small boat without any oars. When they arrived at the shores of Cornwall, in southwest England, King Alfred asked them where they had come from and where they wanted to go. They answered that they "stole away because [they] wanted for the love of God to be on pilgrimage, [they] cared not where."[18] As this story reveals, *peregrinatio* is different from pilgrimages of the Middle Ages. Unlike those pilgrimages, *peregrinatio* does not have a "specific end or goal."[19] While pilgrimage ends with returning home, people who engage in *peregrinatio* allow themselves to be led by the Spirit and are ready to go wherever the Spirit takes them. They consider themselves to be "*hospites mundi*, guests of the world,"[20] seeking "the place of their resurrection, the resurrected self, the true self in Christ."[21] In this way, they try not to become attached to the world.

Various spiritual figures in Celtic Christianity engaged in *peregrinatio*. We have already met St. Columbanus (540–615), considered by De Waal as "one of the greatest of all *peregrini*."[22] He

---

15 de Waal, *The Celtic Way of Prayer*, 2.
16 de Waal, *The Celtic Way of Prayer*, 2.
17 de Waal, *The Celtic Way of Prayer*, 1.
18 de Waal, *The Celtic Way of Prayer*, 2.
19 de Waal, *The Celtic Way of Prayer*, 2.
20 de Waal, *The Celtic Way of Prayer*, 2.
21 de Waal, *The Celtic Way of Prayer*, 2.
22 de Waal, *The Celtic Way of Prayer*, 3.

"spent most of his life wandering across Europe establishing monasteries."[23] As Columbanus' life shows, *peregrinatio* is a costly practice; he died on his journey of wandering as a "stranger and an exile" in the world. He depended entirely on God on his journey and was willing to go wherever God led him.

Likewise well-known is St. Patrick (385–461), "the founding father of the Irish church and one of the foremost Celtic Saints."[24] Patrick is known as an exemplary person who exercised his profound faith even during the trials he encountered. Patrick survived slavery, and even returned to the land in which he had been enslaved to share wisdom and to fight the injustice he had undergone there.[25] He spent the rest of his life in Ireland and dedicated his life entirely to reaching people wherever they resided.

St. Brigid (451–525), a fifth-century abbess of a Celtic monastery, "represents the richness of Celtic hospitality, generosity, and kindness."[26] Carl McColman introduces Brigid as "a figure of inclusivity and hospitality,"[27] for she lived her life embracing others, especially strangers and people in need. One instance of *peregrinatio* occurred during one Lenten season when she and "two other nuns from Kildare" were traveling, and a pagan chieftain invited them in when nightfall came.[28] He served them a meal containing pork, which was forbidden during Lent. While the two nuns protested by saying that they were not allowed to eat the food, Brigid responded: "My apologies, good sir. My sisters are under the mistaken impression that their fast matters more than your hospitality."[29] Caring for others, she believed, is more important than achieving one's personal spiritual goals.

St. Brendan (484–577) engaged in a voyage in which he wandered around the sea for seven years to find "the Island of the Saints."[30] According to McColman, Saint Brendan of Clonfert is his real name and he got the nickname "Brendan the Navigator"[31] due

---

23 Bradley, *The Celtic Way*, 78.
24 Bradley, *The Celtic Way*, 12–13.
25 Carl McColman, *An Invitation to Celtic Wisdom: A Little Guide to Mystery, Spirit, and Compassion* (Charlottesville, VA: Hampton Roads, 2018), 105.
26 McColman, *An Invitation to Celtic Wisdom*, 105.
27 McColman, *An Invitation to Celtic Wisdom*, 90.
28 McColman, *An Invitation to Celtic Wisdom*, 96.
29 McColman, *An Invitation to Celtic Wisdom*, 96–97.
30 Bradley, *The Celtic Way*, 79.
31 McColman, *An Invitation to Celtic Wisdom*, 106.

to this sea voyage. As a wanderer, he embodied Celtic spirituality —
"a deep mystical thirst for God, a thirst to find (and inhabit) heaven
on earth."[32] His voyage covered a wide region "throughout the west
coast of Ireland and journeying to Scotland, Wales, and even
Brittany in mainland Europe,"[33] but his voyage to "the west over the
open sea"[34] was considered the most famous one. In the ancient text
"*Navigatio Sancti Brendani Abbatis — or The Voyage of Saint Brendan*"[35]
the Abbot recorded his voyage.

Columba or Columcille (521–597), "best known as a missionary
to Scotland," should not be excluded from the list of the *peregrini*
since he was exiled. Columba established several monasteries in
Ireland and was renowned as "one of the 'twelve apostles of
Ireland.'"[36] However, he was in trouble for religious and political
issues — due to copying a book of Psalms without the owner's
permission — and it was suggested to him that he go into exile. He
willingly left his home in Ireland and lived in Scotland for the last
thirty-four years of his life, only visiting his homeland again once in
all that time. Columba brought Christianity to Scotland, and among
other things established a monastery on an island, Iona.

The distinctive Celtic Christian spirituality which these spiritual
figures showed was limited during the Middle Ages but
experienced a resurgence in the twentieth century. While Ireland
was disrupted by Viking attacks, "the advent of the Cluniac reforms
in the eleventh century and the Normans in the twelfth...led to the
greater integration of Ireland into the forms and ways of continental
Christianity."[37] Although Celtic Christianity seemed to be diluted in
Continental European Christianity during the Middle Ages, in the
1960s, Celtic spirituality was revived "when a number of paperback
anthologies of prayers started appearing culled largely from the
Carmina Gadelica, the collection of Gaelic prayers, blessings and
incantations collected in the late nineteenth century by Alexander
Carmichael." The writings of "the American monk and spiritual
writer Thomas Merton" and the studies of Scottish theologian John
Macquarrie also contributed to the revival of Celtic spirituality in

---

[32] McColman, *An Invitation to Celtic Wisdom*, 106.
[33] McColman, *An Invitation to Celtic Wisdom*, 106.
[34] McColman, *An Invitation to Celtic Wisdom*, 106.
[35] McColman, *An Invitation to Celtic Wisdom*, 106.
[36] McColman, *An Invitation to Celtic Wisdom*, 118.
[37] Davies and O'Loughlin, *Celtic Spirituality*, 20.

1960s and 1970s.[38] With the publication of a slew of books on Celtic spirituality, such as Robert Van de Weyer's *Celtic Fire* (1990), Esther de Waal's *A World Made Whole: The Rediscovery of the Celtic Tradition* (1991), Edward Sellner's *Wisdom of the Celtic Saints*, and of course Ian Bradley's *The Celtic Way* (1993), Celtic spirituality became increasingly popular.[39] More studies and writings continue to be released to establish Celtic spirituality as one of the distinctive Christian spiritualities today. C.S. Lewis is represented as the twenty-century figure of Celtic spirituality who embodies the concept of pilgrimage, *peregrinatio*. In his book, *The Voyage of the Dawn Treader*, C.S. Lewis illustrates the "life-long project of Christian spirituality."[40]

Indeed, engaging in *peregrinatio*, or sacred wandering as a spiritual practice, has not only been deeply formed by Celtic Christianity but, in turn, has inspired various figures throughout Christian history. As Bradley emphasizes, "Contemporaries saw a commitment to perpetual pilgrimage, exile and wandering as one of the most striking characteristics of the Irish in the early medieval period."[41] How then was *peregrinatio* originally practiced, and how has modern Christianity interpreted the practice for today's context?

The Essential Movements of Peregrinatio

The original form of engaging in peregrinatio has two traditions. The first one is of friends and neighbors of those who depart their homes saying farewell by giving gifts and praying for them. Before they pass through the thresholds of their homes, "a parting hymn would be sung or chanted or intoned or recited in slow, measured cadences."[42] Friends and neighbors of the *peregrini* blessed them with these prayerful words that God, Christ, and the Spirit always protect them wherever they go. Since their journeys require the risk of their lives, the words must have been a desperate or urgent prayer.

---

[38] Bradley, *Following the Celtic Way*, chap. 1.
[39] Bradley, *Following the Celtic Way*, chap. 1.
[40] McColman, *An Invitation to Celtic Wisdom*, 112.
[41] Bradley, *Following the Celtic Way*, chap. 7.
[42] de Waal, *The Celtic Way of Prayer*, 12.

The second tradition was for the persons who take the journey to "bathe their faces with warm milk," especially sheep's milk since it was "sacred to Christ."[43] According to de Waal, bathing represents "purification," and "Mary had bathed her son" when they fled into Egypt.[44] In this way, perhaps they physically experienced and tried to remember God's protection over them. The blessing followed, a blessing seeking God's protection and the presence of God. Depending on the situations and directions of the *peregrini*, they started their journeys either on board a boat or by walking. As soon as they set out on their journeys, they depended fully on God and tried to listen to the Holy Spirit to guide them. Without goals, plans, or maps, they just wandered around the land and the ocean until God spoke, telling them to stay in a particular place. There, they shared the words of God as they were permitted to do so. They lived with their newfound neighbors and engaged in their practices as Christians, but continued to listen to the voice of God concerning when it was time for them to move on to a new place. They sensitively paid attention to God, the One who had been always with them and who speaks through all creation. *Peregrini* were aware that God's presence always accompanied them, and felt "a sense of connectedness with the earth itself."[45] Since they considered God as "the Lord of the elements,"[46] they "[rejoiced] in creation."[47] Of course, they also accepted "the brokenness of the world" and they prayed for God's grace, mercy, and power to save the world.[48] They were attentive to the Holy Spirit to discern when their journey should end. At the end of their journeys, if the *peregrini* returned to their homelands, people celebrated and welcomed them, "glorifying God for not wishing to deprive them any longer of their father who had been away from them for so long."[49] This ancient style of *peregrinatio* requires a huge commitment on the part of family and friends left behind, for one never knew whether the wanderer had died on their journey. One could also not assume they would find a place to stay until God gave them a sign of what to do. Indeed,

[43] de Waal, *The Celtic Way of Prayer*, 13.
[44] de Waal, *The Celtic Way of Prayer*, 13.
[45] de Waal, *The Celtic Way of Prayer*, 16.
[46] de Waal, *The Celtic Way of Prayer*, 17.
[47] de Waal, *The Celtic Way of Prayer*, 23.
[48] de Waal, *The Celtic Way of Prayer*, 23.
[49] Davies and O'Loughlin, *Celtic Spirituality*, 190.

engaging in this type of *peregrinatio* meant and still means offering oneself to God as a living sacrifice, following the Christ who offered his life for us. That is why this ancient form of *peregrinatio* was not and is not broadly practiced, and was largely the practice of persons such as monks.

Donald McKinney, author of *Walking the Mist: Celtic Spirituality for the 21st Century*, proposes a form of *peregrinatio* more applicable for people today.[50] In comparison with the ancient one, this modern type of practice is a very much shorter version of *peregrinatio*, and one which does not require a huge commitment of one's life. At the beginning of *peregrinatio*, according to McKinney's suggestion, participants can interpret for themselves the signs that tell them to start their journeys. Then, they simply sit down or engage in meditation. As they feel moved, they begin to walk onto the path, or to wherever their Spirit-led journey takes them, remaining attuned to their surroundings and to the Spirit. In that sacred moment, the participants let the Spirit guide them and soak in the moment. As the Spirit brings them back to where their bodies are, they can be themselves again and be aware of their bodies. McKinney insists that the practice helps to block the participants' inner thoughts, worries, or dividedness. He defines this practice as "a Celtic pilgrimage [that is] a walk into awareness."[51]

McKinney suggests that individuals engage in a daylong or even longer pilgrimage. To set out on this kind of pilgrimage, the participants prepare ahead of time by setting a specific day or time for their journey. As they begin the practice, McKinney suggests that they can use their common sense and that it is better not to worry about where they will go. This is the essential point of engaging in *peregrinatio*: as in its ancient form, participants try their best to be led by God by paying attention to the voice of God. At the same time, as they walk, they become aware of their surroundings, including trees, animals, insects, and so on. In short, the practice invites them to contemplate their surroundings and the presence of God. He warns them not to stick to their own expectations but to wander around places. When they feel the desire to return to their homes, common sense will tell them to finish their journeys.

---

[50] Donald McKinney, *Walking the Mist: Celtic Spirituality for the 21st Century* (London: Hodder Mobius, 2004), 76.
[51] McKinney, *Walking the Mist*, 77.

The Purposes and Outcomes of Peregrinatio

McKinney describes the purpose of the Celtic pilgrimage or *peregrinatio* as submerging oneself "into the world of nature and spirit, to leave the material world far behind."[52] It means to leave our familiar places and give ourselves over to the creation that holds God's presence. Thus, since *peregrinatio* involves physical movement, the concept of physical incarnation is a crucial part of being fully immersed in nature and the spirit. Through this physical involvement, *peregrinatio* enables us to accept the fact that we are living in this world, on earth. In other words, through it, people can become more present and one with nature and God. Indeed, de Waal suggests that this emphasis on flesh helps people to accept more fully their own humanity.[53]

Celts considered it eminently worthwhile to meditate on all elements of nature, such as the sun, wind, earth, water, and flowers.[54] Thus, Celtic theology emphasizes "the essential goodness of nature, including human nature, and s[ees] Jesus Christ as the one who was sent not so much to rescue the world from the consequences of the fall as to complete and perfect it."[55] Theologically, this viewpoint was influenced by Pelagianism, which stresses the original goodness of all created beings, including nature and human beings. Thus, Christ came to earth to perfect or complete those created beings.[56] Ian Bradley finds three reasons why Celtic Christianity agrees with the goodness of creation: 1) biblical roots tell us there are many things to celebrate in God; 2) "the Druid nature mysticism," which worshiped nature; 3) the beautiful nature in which they lived.[57] Although *peregrinatio* celebrates God in all created beings, it tends to deny the flesh.

Ian Bradley, the author of *The Celtic Way*, asserts that *peregrinatio* was Celtic Christians' chosen form of asceticism, through which they were perpetually exiled "from the comforts and distractions of

---

[52] McKinney, *Walking the Mist*, 75–76.
[53] de Waal, *The Celtic Way of Prayer*, 24.
[54] Edward J. Farrell, *Celtic Meditations: Moments of Thanksgiving, Invitations to Eucharist* (Denville, NJ: Dimension Books, 1976).
[55] Bradley, *The Celtic Way*, 52.
[56] Bradley, *The Celtic Way*, 52.
[57] Bradley, *The Celtic Way*, 53–54.

home."[58] In order to achieve their spiritual goals to follow Jesus and deny themselves, they left their safe, comfortable, and loving homeland. Some pilgrims even walked barefoot.[59] This intention of asceticism is to follow Jesus Christ who came on earth as an exile. Bradley expresses this as the "desire to follow the path of renunciation and self-denial."[60] Bradley also explains that "to be a pilgrim was to live in imitation of Jesus, to take up his cross and to recognize that in this transitory world we have no abiding city."[61] Indeed, their apocalyptic perspective reinforced the rule not to have their hearts settled on earth, as their place to live. Of course, creating the kingdom of heaven on earth is still important for their lives, so they tried to find God within themselves and others via their interior journey.

Thus, finding God and oneself in others can be an outcome of *peregrinatio*. According to de Waal, this practice is about finding God's presence and Christ within others.[62] She goes on to say that it is about finding oneself as well, that people can accept the fact that living in this world is an endless journey and is about "becoming a more loving person."[63] Indeed, as de Waal claims, the Celtic way of prayer can be considered as a "journey into prayer." She notes that "It is *peregrinatio*, seeking, quest, adventure, wandering, exile — it is ultimately a journey...to find the place of my resurrection, the resurrected self, the self that I might hope to be, to become, the true self in Christ."[64] Via *peregrinatio*, one can take one's journey into prayer, and this wandering helps one to find oneself in Christ.

The process of finding God and Christ in oneself and others generates compassion. As *peregrini* are connected with God, the source of compassion, they can cultivate love for themselves as well as others. Various *peregrini* showed their love toward others, a love that stemmed from their love for God and themselves. They offered their lives for strangers by living with them, provided the needs of *peregrini*, forgave their enemies with God's love, and even lived with them the rest of their lives. Today, the compassion practice of the

---

[58] Bradley, *The Celtic Way*, 77.
[59] McKinney, *Walking the Mist*, 80.
[60] Bradley, *The Celtic Way*, 77.
[61] Bradley, *The Celtic Way*, 81.
[62] de Waal, *The Celtic Way of Prayer*, 26.
[63] deWaal, *The Celtic Way of Prayer*, 27.
[64] de Waal, ix.

Center for Engaged Compassion, developed by Frank Rogers Jr., embodies what *peregrinatio* seeks, the way of Jesus: loving our neighbors as ourselves (Matthew 22:39).

Spiritual Insights and Wisdom from Peregrinatio

Peregrinatio gives a spiritual framework and consolation to those who live as immigrants, exiles, and strangers—and there increasingly many of us like this today. Although people often voluntarily choose to live in other countries, it is not always easy for them to find stability or a sense of belonging in that new place. And once one has moved, one often feels like a stranger back in one's home culture. Asian American practical theologian Courtney T. Goto recognizes this sense or state of "in-between" in "Asian American Practical Theologies."[65] Goto insists that while this state of in-between does often cause "suffering and alienation," it is also a creative space.[66] I know that from experience. As the wife of a Korean international student, the mother of Korean American kid, and as a Korean international student myself, I have experienced myself as a stranger in the United States for eleven years. Unlike other Korean immigrants in the U.S. who are willing to be fully absorbed into the new land and its culture, international students like me usually plan to return to their home countries after their studies.[67] Thus, while I lived in the U.S., I felt as if my family and I were living in a liminal space. Bearing in mind Goto's suggestion, however, the spirituality of *peregrinatio* has given me a spiritual framework by which to understand that being a stranger, immigrant, or exile does not have to be a negative state. Rather, it is the natural state of all human beings as Anselm Grün, who studies a theology of wandering, emphasizes that human beings are

---

[65] Courtney T. Goto, "Asian American Practical Theologies," in *Opening the Field of Practical Theology: An Introduction*, ed. Kathleen A. Cahalan and Gordon S. Mikoski (Lanham: Rowman & Littlefield Publishers, 2014), 41.

[66] Goto, "Asian American Practical Theologies," 41.

[67] Most of the early Korean immigrants tended to be absorbed into the society of the United States. For example, they abandoned their original religions, and faithful Korean immigrants interpreted and believed their journeys as a pilgrimage that they responded to God's calling to live in the United States as total immigrants. Su Yon Pak et al., *Singing the Lord's Song in a New Land: Korean American Practices of Faith* (Louisville, KY: Westminster John Knox Press, 2005), 3–11.

intrinsically wanderers, foreigners, and strangers.[68] As Grün observes, the earth is a foreign land for all human beings that we have our eternal home in the heaven, and since the original sin, we became exiles. Thus, human beings must wander around the earth while we are living in this world. This consoles my soul that I was not the only one who wanders around the world. The spirituality of *peregrinatio* focuses on Jesus Christ's being as a stranger on earth. The life of Jesus, from his birth to death, shows his journey on the road. Christ invites his followers to his path by leaving behind what we used to attach, denying ourselves, and taking up our crosses to follow Christ. This calling was the motivation of *peregrini* who followed this path of Christ physically and spiritually. Like *peregrini*, my husband and I decided to study theology in the U.S. to follow Christ more closely, and then returned to Korea after we finished our studies responding to God's sign to return. Thus, I interpret my life while I was studying in the U.S. as *peregrinatio*, and even now I open myself to continuously be a *peregrina*. Indeed, the spirit of *peregrinatio*, helps people who identify themselves as immigrants, exiles, or strangers to see their lives as *peregrini*, gives consolation that they are not the only people who wander around the world and confirm their lives as followers of Christ.

Peregrinatio starts with and involves in an inward journey. In this journey, *peregrini* can take care of the interior world and find the true selves in Christ. As de Waal emphasizes, *peregrini* expressed their inward journeys outwardly.[69] *Peregrini* set out their journeys with their love of Christ. Although they physically started their journeys at some point, they already were in their journey in their mind. Celtic monks considered themselves as pilgrims whether they stay in their hermit cells or take their journey as *peregrini*. The spirit of *peregrinatio* turns our attention to the kingdom of heaven. As the initial inward movement, by leaving behind their homes, families, and possessions to set out the actual journey, *peregrini* could start to detach from their attachment. Thus, they confirmed their being as "*hospites mundi*, guests of the world."[70] Since *peregrini* did not have any possessions, plans, or destinations, they must fully be relied on

---

[68] Anselm Grün, *Auf dem Wege: Zu einer Theologie des Wanderns*, translated by Young-Ryong Kim, 길 위에서: 그리스도인을 위한 걷기의 신학, (Benedict Press, Waegwan, Korea, 2020), 22-23.
[69] de Waal, *The Celtic Way of Prayer*, 2.
[70] de Waal, *The Celtic Way of Prayer*, 2.

God's help and guidance. Thus, they needed to be still and silence to pay attention to God's direction. In this state of silence, when *peregrini* walked into their awareness, they are invited to take an inward journey to get rid of any obstacles to encounter the presence of God and to be fully their true self in Christ.

This interior journey of *peregrinatio* invites us to allow unfamiliarity in our lives, including other human beings. When living or wandering in foreign lands, wanderers are invited not only to allow themselves to be absorbed into the lands but also to accept the unfamiliarity that comes toward them. Their intention to follow the path of Jesus, the path of radical compassion, makes this possible. The story of St. Brigid's encounter with a pagan chieftain's strange dinner table during Lent season well illustrates the importance of receiving kindness from a stranger, regardless of their religious determination. St. Patrick embraced the people and the land, although he suffered in Ireland at a young age. He even had compassion toward them, so he decided to return to the land to live for the rest of his life. Although wandering in strange lands and allowing strangers in our lives is risky, the spirit of *peregrinatio* encourages us to fully be present in the moment where we are and embrace as gifts whatever comes to us. Therefore, we can become more loving persons, as de Waal emphasizes.[71]

The Applications of Peregrinatio

Peregrinatio can be adapted and implemented in various ways, depending on the time, distance, or degree of engagement available to the practitioner. It can be a twenty-minute-long walking meditation that participants take along unfamiliar roads. It can be a long journey on which participants go wherever God leads them and return to their homes whenever they are ready or receive a sign from God. It can be a lifelong journey for those who feel called to leave their homes permanently, as Abraham did. *Peregrinatio* can even refer to studying abroad as an international student, living in different countries as an immigrant, or being involved in mission fields as a missionary. Regardless of the reasons, people can consider their lives as *peregrinatio* if they recognize themselves as wanderers who follow the path of Jesus and seek the kingdom of

---

[71] deWaal, *The Celtic Way of Prayer*, 27.

heaven. *Peregrinatio* can be integrated into other forms of spiritual practices such as walking meditation, compassion practice, and other contemplative practices. Visiting retreat centers would be another form of *peregrinatio* in which participants leave their homes for a time to engage fully in this practice and to tend their interior life.

Peregrinatio can be an appropriate contemplative walking practice for Christians today because people love walking, especially in nature, and many already engage in walking as a daily practice. Some people engage in walking meditation as their daily spiritual practice. Such modern forms of *peregrinatio* do not require a lifelong commitment, and people can engage in this short version of *peregrinatio* relatively easily as a part of their daily lives. The time and place of the practice can be flexible, depending on participants' intentions or purposes. In this modern type of short *peregrinatio*, people will typically not need to worry about whether they are lost. Still, it is important to keep the attitude of the original *peregrinatio* and rely fully on God's guidance by establishing no hard and fast destination or purpose for one's wandering. Through engaging in this modern type of *peregrinatio*, people can become more present to themselves, to others, to God, and to the world. As Farrell describes, "Walking is a kind of seeing, a kind of feeling, a kind of being present, rendering oneself present."[72] As we walk along the streets, trails, or gardens, we learn to see our surroundings. We have to see, otherwise we will get into trouble. We need to see where we are going, and our sight can be one of the main pathways through which to sense our present moment. As we contemplate our surroundings, we can feel and notice that our feet touch the ground, that our noses and mouths breathe in and out the fresh air, the presence of God. The more we see and feel where we are, the more we become present. As we touch the ground, we become aware of ourselves and what it means to be alive in this very moment, with the result that we live more fully.

The compassion practice of the Center for Engaged Compassion embodies the spirituality of *peregrinatio* and people can engage in the compassion practice as their inner journey or integrate it while they are engaging in outer *peregrinatio*. *In Compassion in Practice: The*

---

[72] Edward J. Farrell, *Celtic Meditations: Moments of Thanksgiving, Invitations to Eucharist* (Denville, NJ: Dimension Books, 1976), 92.

Way of Jesus, Frank Rogers Jr. suggests how to cultivate compassion. Although people may be able to feel compassion most of the time, they sometimes experience a blocking of compassion that often derives from "drivenness or hyper-reactivity."[73] For that reason, people need to cultivate their compassion. To Rogers, compassion is metaphorically "a movement of the heart" and "a heartbeat of compassion,"[74] which has six dimensions. The first dimension is "paying attention": compassion requires seeing others with "contemplative awareness."[75] The second dimension is "understanding empathically": compassion entails being moved by the pain and joy of others.[76] The third dimension is "loving with connection": compassion includes "nonjudgmental, all-embracing, infinitely loving quality of presence."[77] The fourth dimension is "sensing the sacredness": compassion is considered "a spiritual energy."[78] The fifth dimension is "embodying new life": compassion "yearns for the transformation of suffering into joy."[79] The sixth dimension is acting: compassion requires restorative action for the flourishing of others. As Rogers emphasizes, "Without action, compassion becomes sentimentality"[80] that we need to embody our compassion for ourselves and others through the genuine act of compassion.

On the basis of the essential components of compassion, Rogers offers a fourfold rhythm of Jesus' path of compassion. The first movement is to "catch your breath," in which people "take a deep breath" in order to "get grounded"[81] and to reconnect to the source of compassion, God. This can entail taking a literal deep breath or a short *peregrinatio*–taking a walk, preferably in nature, and reminding ourselves of the presence of God. My daily walking contemplative practice was one of the ways in which I reconnected to the source of God when I studied in the U.S. as an international student. I recharged my spiritual battery by catching my breath. The

---

[73] Rogers, *Compassion in Practice,* 35.

[74] Rogers, *Compassion in Practice,* 30.

[75] Rogers, *Compassion in Practice,* 30–31.

[76] Rogers, *Compassion in Practice,* 31.

[77] Rogers, *Compassion in Practice,* 32.

[78] Rogers, *Compassion in Practice,* 32.

[79] Rogers, *Compassion in Practice,* 33. Rogers made an acronym — PULSE — from the five essential movements.

[80] Rogers, *Compassion in Practice,*115.

[81] Rogers, *Compassion in Practice,* 35.

second movement is to "take your PULSE," in which people "take a U-turn... look inward, and... recalibrate [their] pulse to the steady heartbeat of humanity," in order to restore their compassionate selves.[82] *Peregrinatio* involves this inward journey to take care of the inner movements that hinder us from reconnecting to God and being our true self in Christ. Through taking my pulse, I became aware of my various inner movements, such as anxiety, bitterness, and a sense of alienation as a foreigner. The third movement is to "take the other's PULSE," in which people "[connect] with the PULSE of humanity beating within [others]"[83] with the same essential components of compassion mentioned in the second movement. Just as Celtic Christianity affirms the goodness of all created beings, so too compassion practice acknowledges that we all are created in the image of God, compassion, so we all have our innate compassion. Though they made him suffer, St. Patrick tried to understand people by finding the image of God within them. In the context of U.S. where countless ethnic groups live together, understanding or embracing others is not always easy. However, taking the pulse of others can be an effective movement or way to understand and have compassion for others. The fourth movement is to "decide what to do," in which people "discern compassionate action."[84] As I mentioned above, Rogers strongly highlights the action of compassion to ease the suffering and to seek the flourishing of others. St. Brigid might have engaged such a process to discern what to do when the other two nuns refused the feast of the pagan chieftain. She then decided to loosen her adherence to a particular religious practice for a moment, recognized the innate goodness of the strangers, and partook in the forbidden foods.

Indeed, the compassion practice aligns with the spirituality of *peregrinatio* and offers us a practical and concrete way to cultivate and embody compassion in our lives today. When we practice either inner or outer *peregrinatio* through this compassion practice, we can find our true self in Christ and become more loving persons.

As a distinctive spiritual practice in Celtic Christianity, *peregrinatio* has been practiced throughout the Christian history. Although this practice seemed not to have been actively practiced

---

[82] Rogers, *Compassion in Practice*, 36.
[83] Rogers, *Compassion in Practice*, 37.
[84] Rogers, *Compassion in Practice*, 39.

during the Middle Ages, thanks to the revival of Celtic spirituality in 1960s *peregrinatio* has been re-emerged as a powerful spiritual practice. The spirituality of *peregrinatio* inspires and consoles Christians who dwell in and wander in foreign lands as immigrants, exiles, or strangers. By re-framing their lives through the framework of *peregrinatio*, we see them afresh as followers of Christ who lived on earth as an exile. As long as they seek God's guidance and will in their lives, they are *peregrini* who are searching for the kingdom of heaven. While journeying outwardly, this journey also involves an inward journey to encounter the presence of God and to take care of our inner worlds. *Peregrinatio* invites us to embrace unfamiliarity in our lives, to be more present, and to become more loving persons. As we integrate *peregrinatio* into our daily walking practice and the compassion practice, we are exposed to the light of God, the source of compassion, in our daily lives.

Bibliography

Bradley, Ian. *Following the Celtic Way: A New Assessment of Celtic Christianity*. Augsburg Books, 2020. Kindle.

— — —. *The Celtic Way*. London: Darton, Longman and Todd, 1993.

Chadwick, Nora Kershaw. *The Celts*. Penguin Books, 1991.

Davies, Oliver, and Thomas. O'Loughlin. *Celtic Spirituality*. The Classics of Western Spirituality. New York: Paulist Press, 1999.

de Waal, Esther. *The Celtic Way of Prayer*. New York: Doubleday, 1997.

Farrell, Edward J. *Celtic Meditations: Moments of Thanksgiving, Invitations to Eucharist*. Denville, NJ: Dimension Books, 1976.

Goto, Courtney T. "Asian American Practical Theologies." In *Opening the Field of Practical Theology: An Introduction*, edited by Kathleen A. Cahalan and Gordon S. Mikoski, 31–44. Lanham, MD: Rowman & Littlefield Publishers, 2014.

Grün, Anselm, *Auf dem Wege: Zu einer Theologie des Wanderns*, translated by Young-Ryong Kim, 길 위에서: 그리스도인을 위한 걷기의 신학. Benedict Press, Waegwan, Korea, 2020.

McColman, Carl. *An Invitation to Celtic Wisdom: A Little Guide to Mystery, Spirit, and Compassion*. Charlottesville: Hampton Roads, 2018.

McKinney, Donald. *Walking the Mist: Celtic Spirituality for the 21st Century*. London: Hodder Mobius, 2004.

Mursell, Gordon. *The Story of Christian Spirituality: Two Thousand Years, from East to West*. Minneapolis, MN: Fortress Press, 2001.

Rogers, Frank, Jr. *Compassion in Practice: The Way of Jesus*. Nashville, TN: Upper Room Books, 2016.

To Be Known as Beloved: The Welcoming Presence and Radical Hospitality of the Compassion Practice

Catherine Wilson

Imagine a space where *all is held,* where you are *beloved.* This is the space of the Compassion Practice, embodied in radical hospitality and acceptance. This is the work of Frank Rogers, Jr. The unique facets of Rogers' formulation of engaged compassion-based practices through such concepts as radical hospitality, self-compassion, a non-pathologizing and accepting stance toward interior movements, the role of story and personal narrative, and the invitation to welcome a sacred presence into one's midst are described in this chapter. The chapter focuses on three primary areas: An overview of Rogers' formulation and practice of engaged compassion-based practices; the unique characteristics of Rogers' formulation of engaged compassion-based practices which position these practices as highly adaptable for any number of practical applications; and examples from "The Goddess Finishing School" program curriculum that are illustrative of the positive role these practices play in the spiritual/emotional/psycho-social development of female-identifying individuals– particularly with respect to self-compassion, sense of self, agency, resilience, authenticity, relationality, and a sense of community.

As a member of the Religious Society of Friends (Quakers), I believe that *all* persons deserve respect, support, life-giving and flourishing growth, positive sense of self, authenticity, hope, agency, and empowerment. It is my belief that we can learn and apply practices to support these goals. It is from this location and context as a middle-aged, upper middle-class, Friend, mother, feminist, and practical theologian that I have grounded my engagement in this work. I have not always occupied my current place of privilege. A survivor of a chaotic and often violent childhood home, child sexual abuse, and domestic violence, I was once a youth on the margins. I distinctly remember thinking; *I must be completely worthless or else someone would try to do something.* It is my conviction that if *one* caring adult or mentor had intervened, I might have avoided some of my dangerous behavior and pain.[1] My research interests spring from a deep leading to *be* that one caring adult and to contribute a program to assist others in doing the same. Frank Rogers is the mentor I yearned for as a young person—always encouraging, offering guidance and feedback that is generous and constructive, and setting the example with extravagant compassionate and ethical action. I learned from Frank a way of being and practices that have transformed my life. As a Friend, all of my work centers on an ongoing, *lived* experience of the D/divine. As such, my starting point is always experiential and praxis-based.

The Compassion Practice

The Compassion Practice, developed by Frank Rogers, Jr., Andrew Dreitcer, and Mark Yaconelli of the Center for Engaged Compassion at Claremont School of Theology, draws from the world's wisdom traditions and contemplative practices. The Compassion Practice is based on these traditions' universal, though varying, foundational beliefs that compassion is inherent in the heart of all beings—from the beliefs and concepts of Buddhists' *lovingkindness*, to the Christian Golden Rule: *do unto others as you would have done unto you*, to Rabbi Hilel's "Do not do that which you find harmful to yourself, unto anyone else. That is the whole of Torah, the rest is commentary."[2] Further, the Compassion Practice is grounded on the concept, also common to all wisdom traditions, of humans' intrinsic goodness—such as Quakers' belief in *that which is God is within everyone*, also known as *the Light within*; the Buddhists' *Buddha self*; and the Christian *imago dei*. When we can connect to and be grounded in this inherent state of compassion, we can be true to ourselves and others, and we can operate and exist in our world from a place of grounded Self-Leadership.[3]

---

[1] See for example, Bessel van der Kolk's discussion on social support, safety, and reciprocity in *The Body Keeps the Score: Brain, Mind, and Body in the Healing of Trauma* (New York: Penguin, 2014), 81.

[2] Richard R. Osmer, *Practical Theology: An Introduction* (Grand Rapids: Wm. B. Eerdmans Publishing Co., 2008), 4.

[3] Self-Leadership is a concept of Richard C. Schwartz's theory of Internal Family Systems, in which Schwartz applied family systems theory to one's internal landscape. Schwartz applied those principles to the *internal* worlds of his patients,

Rogers defines compassion as "being moved in one's depths by another's experience, and responding in a way that intends either to ease their suffering or promote their flourishing."[4] The Compassion Practice draws heavily on the teachings of the radical Jesus. This is the Jesus whose love was all-accepting, all encompassing, who fought for social justice and for those who were persecuted. The compassion of Jesus calls for unconditional love, but also stands non-violently and creatively against oppressive forces and structures. The Compassion Practice is not one that advocates for passivity, but for courage, dignity, empowerment, and respect. We can see Jesus' imprint on the Compassion Practice by the very names of some of its practices, such as *on the mountain* in which one retreats from the world to a place of contemplation in order to reconnect to one's grounded self and a sacred presence much like Jesus' practice of contemplative retreat. The counterpart to the *on the mountain* practices are *in the moment* practices, designed to be called upon to bring a grounded presence to a difficult situation at hand.

The Compassion Practice is situated in the discipline of practical theology and the science of contemplative practices and, as Andrew Dreitcer, co-founder with Frank Rogers, Jr., of the Center for Engaged Compassion, asserts in *Living Compassion: Loving Like Jesus*, radical compassion can be taught. Dreitcer states that "in the Bible, genuine compassion contains three characteristics that inseparably intertwine: understanding, feeling, and acting."[5] To follow is the basic structure of the Compassion Practice.

The Basic Structure of The Compassion Practice

Dreitcer examines the components of the Compassion Practice in *Living Compassion: Loving Like Jesus*. When the Compassion Practice was in its nascent form, Dreitcer and Yaconelli were intrigued to observe their friend, Rogers, as he engaged with his personal, spiritual practice. Dreitcer and Yaconelli sought to deconstruct Rogers' process and its movements, including the practice's invitation to return to one's inner movements and tend to

---

applying the term *Parts* to refer to one's complex internal landscape with the conviction that all *Parts* have a positive intention for the individual.
[4] Frank Rogers, Jr., *Practicing Compassion* (Nashville, TN: Upper Room, 2015), 23.
[5] Andrew Dreitcer, *Living Compassion: Loving like Jesus* (Nashville: Upper Room Books, 2017), 22.

them, counter to the movements of many other spiritual practices. The result of this unique engagement with the practical theological cycle of *practice, reflection, practice* is the Compassion Practice.

The Compassion Practice follows four steps which invite the practitioner to connect with the D/divine, or Sacred Source; become grounded; cultivate a deep connection and relationship with the D/divine, self, and others; and, finally, to engage in a process of discernment of compassionate action:

1. Catch your breath (Get grounded). Get some emotional and physical distance in whatever ways help you become centered and reconnected with the source of your vitality.
2. Take your PULSE (Cultivate compassion for yourself). Take a U-turn and connect empathically with the cry of your soul hidden within your emotions and impulses.
3. Take the other's PULSE (Cultivate compassion for another). Turn toward the other and connect empathically with the cry of the soul hidden within his or her emotions and behaviors.
4. Decide what to do (Discern compassionate action). Now grounded in compassion — both for yourself and the other — discern those actions that heal the suffering and nurture the flourishing of all parties involved and do them.[6]

Taking one's PULSE includes the following steps:

P – Pay Attention (contemplative awareness)

U – Understand Empathically (sense what is going on under the surface)

L – Loving Connection (soften to a loving connection with self or others)

S – Sense the Sacred (this is a spiritual practice, invite the D/divine's presence)

E – Embody New Life (a desire for flourishing)

Dreitcer notes a key difference of the Compassion Practice from other compassion cultivation practices regarding feelings and interior movements: "Other practice traditions take a second approach. They try to ignore or stamp out so-called negative

---

[6] Rogers, *Practicing Compassion*,19.

feelings (such as fear, anger, and jealousy), while they encourage those they see as 'positive' (including joy, gratitude, and empathy)." The Compassion Practice, however, follows an "… ultimately more helpful path for forming compassion. They treat all feelings, whether positive or negative, as fertile soil for growing compassion. This approach combines ancient spiritual wisdom with current neuroscientific understandings of emotion."[7] Indeed, returning as often as necessary to tend our interior movements is a distinctive difference of the Compassion Practice. Another distinguishing characteristic of the Compassion Practice is the notion that our interior movements present themselves with positive intentions for us.

Within the Compassion Practice, in addition to working directly with interior movements or our *Parts*, befriending them and working to ease their burdens, we practice self-compassion by taking the *U-Turn* in which we continually come back to tend those interior movements/*Parts* before extending compassion to the other.[8] When engaging with the Compassion Practice and we are not fully in the calm, curious, compassionate space of Self, we can practice the FLAG as part of the U-Turn invitation.[9] In the FLAG practice, once grounded, we ask: *What is my Fear? What is my Longing? What is my Aching Wound? What is my Gift wanting to be expressed?* We go through this series for ourselves, and then — if ready — we extend the same creative practice to the *other*. If we're not open to the other, we practice the U-Turn and FLAG again until our interior movements relax, and we feel ourselves soften into openness and compassion.

The Compassion Practice is suited for, and has been applied to, a variety of settings, such as social activism, work with the incarcerated, difficult conversations about race, in the workplace, work with victims/survivors of trauma and those experiencing secondary trauma, and those experiencing grief.[10] My focus brings

---

[7] Dreitcer, *Living Compassion*, 42.

[8] Tom Holmes' drawings and text illustrate the inner emotional and psychological world in *Parts Work: An Illustrated Guide to Your Inner Life*.

[9] The FLAG practice is my go-to practice, one that I have found can be worked *in the moment* and *on the mountain* to astonishingly positive effect.

[10] See for example Alane Daugherty's *The Power Within: From Neuroscience to Transformation; From Mindfulness to Heartfulness: A Journey of Transformation*

the Compassion Practice to my work with those who identify as girls and young women.

Distinguishing Elements of Compassion Formation in the Compassion Practice

Much of my own compassion formation instruction is unique to the pedagogy of the faculty Claremont School of Theology and the Center for Engaged Compassion. This formation is distinct from other compassion formation programs. The following are the principal distinctions of the manner in which the Claremont School of Theology and the Center for Engaged Compassion cultivate compassion:

1. Response to One's Interior Life: Even in the way we practice compassion cultivation, we are always invited to befriend and tend to the internal landscape. Other models, for example, call for a practice of releasing–*notice what's going on, be kind to it, then release it.* A major distinction of Rogers' formulation is *tending to, taking the U-turn* and *befriending and understanding that* our interior movements, our *Parts* are all protective and have a positive intention for us. In the *Goddess Finishing School* program, I used the buoy analogy: if, in response to our internal movements, we push them down, then, as long as we apply pressure, it stays down. But, once we let up on the pressure, whatever we have been holding down is going to come back up. On the other hand, if it comes up and we befriend and tend to it, it will relax, providing us with the space and mindset to better understand the underlying concern, and to attend to that. That's distinctly, uniquely Frank Roger's contribution–to keep coming back to, befriending, and not demonizing our internal movements. By taking a non-pathologizing stance toward our internal movements, we are able to gain a better understanding of ourselves and develop the skill to return to these practices in times of distress.

2. Radical Hospitality and A Spirit of Always saying *Yes*. The philosophical and pedagogical approaches of Frank Rogers and the

---

Through the Science of Embodiment; and *Unstressed: How Somatic Awareness Can Transform Your Body's Stress Response and Build Emotional Resilience* and Christopher Carter's *The Spirit of Soul Food: Race, Faith, and Food Justice.*

faculty and staff of Claremont School of Theology are those of inclusivity, radical acceptance, and hospitality. Instead of saying *no, you've got to fit into an established methodology, you're not doing the practice right, you've got to sit this way*, it's always *okay*, whatever is coming up, there's a reason, so always say *yes* and try to understand it. With this acceptance comes the invitation to bring out the goodness within the interior movement, employing *radical trust*. As a personal example, I was told as a young person that I was too stupid to be anything. To show up at CST and meet Frank Rogers and the dean of admissions at the time, Jennifer Hooten, was life-changing. They were so friendly, welcoming, and affirming. They said *you're just the person for CST, we see all that you will contribute to this community.* This openness and real hospitality are hallmarks of the compassion cultivation and spiritual formation program at Claremont School of Theology. In speaking with my current colleagues in my professional life, I realize how extraordinary this is. I don't know that I would have pursued a graduate education had Frank Rogers and Jennifer Hooten not been my first introduction to Claremont School of Theology.

The Goddess Finishing School curriculum follows a hermeneutic of radical hospitality, in making a space where *all are welcome*, intentionally setting about to make the physical space open, welcoming, and safe (enough). Helping to create *safe enough space* for participants is another aspect of radical hospitality. This is achieved in part, through working with the group to develop a covenant for the group's work together, in which mutual guidelines are agreed upon. For example, *The Goddess Finishing School* pilot session included time to review the plans for the session; participants' personal introductions, sharing about themselves; a collaborative setting of intentions; and participatory development of guiding principles which were then posted on the wall. My original suggestions used as a starting point for the development of the group covenant were as follows:

- Confidentiality
  - *Reasonable Confidentiality — explain concept*
- Listen with open mind and heart, nonjudgmental
- You can opt in/out throughout as you feel comfortable
- No cross talk
- No advice giving or fixing

117

- Space for Introverts and Extroverts (not taking up all the space in the room)
- Diversity
- We all come with our own stories, be respectful of one another's story
- This is where the group landed as their set of guiding principles:
- Be Kind
- Be nonjudgmental
- Confidentiality
- Speak from own experience (no "spilling of the tea"– gossiping)

3. Uniqueness of the Practices: The compassion formation practices as formulated by Frank Rogers and the Claremont School of Theology and Center for Engaged Compassion programs emphasize our relationship to self. These practices focus on tending and befriending, not releasing and distancing. It is in turning inward, that we are then able to turn (extend) outward, to connect with common humanity.

Because of my belief in the importance of embodied practices with the participants. the Body Scan practice was one of the unique practices of *The Goddess Finishing School* pilot. To follow is a partial transcript from the post-practice and debrief:

Post Practice, immediately following practice (facilitator):
When you're ready, just roll to one side, and just really take your time. Imagine it's a Saturday morning and you don't have to get up and rush to school...Think about your experience of the practice. Notice if there's anything you want to remember about how you feel right now so that you can come back to a practice like this anytime. Remember what it feels like in your body. And when you bring this conscious awareness to how you're feeling, this helps you to cement the state of being so that you can more easily access it at other times. And if you practice it regularly–whatever kind of practice works best for you, if you practice regularly, then when you do have an upsetting situation, you can more easily get back to this place. So, again, just gently think if there's anything you want to remember from this.

118

The participants then took a break in order to provide time for them to process their experience. A snack of home-made baked goods and fruit was served after the break (radical hospitality).

Post Practice Debrief (facilitator):

Why embodied practices? Our bodies sense and process before our brain does. We can learn to pay attention to our body, heed its signals to us, have tools to understand and address our needs. The point I want to make about embodiment is, literally, we live in our bodies, and it's important to remember how important it is to be connected to and responsive to our bodies. Our body senses things often before our brain can process information. You know that feeling when we say *my gut tells me?* Or, another example is, if we're on a hike, and we see something up ahead on the path, our body might register alarm before our brain has the time to process *Is that a snake, or just a stick?* Additionally, with so many external cultural and media pressures on the appearance of girls and women—it's important to have a strong connection and sense of your own body. We live in our bodies. And also, as girls and young women or older women–as females–we have a lot of different pressures on us, from ourselves, from culture. And so, it's really important to be in and aware of our bodies. Just to think about our bodies gives us a lot of information often sooner than our brains do. When we have the ability to check in with our body, you know how we say like 'that just doesn't feel right in my gut'? That's all of our body systems giving us information often before our brain can process it.

Participant Debrief Comments:

Okay. Anyway, so I personally—yoga used to not be my thing. I would be like, "what's the point in just sitting and like stretching?" And that was my philosophy before. And then, for some reason today, I'm not sure why, my body just really relaxed, and it was so— it was like, "Well, I'm really relaxed. (Participant)

And so, I think that's why today was so, so different and so new and amazing because you got to really relax and really feel the value, having that mindfulness time. (Participant)

119

We then spent time as a group for the participants to share which activities they engage in to relax and to gain a sense of calm. The primary reason for this exercise was to point out to the participants that they already engage in *embodied contemplative practices*.

4. Narrative Approach: As opposed to an intellectual understanding of the concept of interconnection, the compassion formation practices developed by Frank Rogers, help people to *feel* the story in order to promote awareness and understanding. An example of this is my personal *Mama Duck and Her Ducklings* story that I use in my compassion sessions with youth in which recount an occasion in which I stopped traffic on a suburban street in order for a mama duck and her ducklings to cross the road. Uncharacteristic of a group of people stopped in traffic, once the line of delayed motorists realized the purpose of my actions, they cheered and hooted for the ducks, one going so far as to say, *Good for you! Good for the ducks! Good for all of us!* Hearing the story, you're moved by a small act of kind action. When participants are moved and in a receptive state, we can use this example as a way to develop an understanding of compassion toward ourselves–we hear the story underneath, that of the inner movements of the Parts. From there, we can move toward teaching how to cultivate compassion for another: in hearing the story and paying attention to whatever is going on underneath we can then emotionally and effectively connect with the other's story in a way that is open-hearted and compassionate as well as non-self-negating. Another example: as a means of explaining Nonviolent Communication (NVC)[11] in *The Goddess Finishing School* pilot, I took a narrative approach, retelling a story of my use of the model in a difficult conversation with police officers after an incident of vandalism at my home. The participants were enthralled by my real-life story and were excited to then practice the NVC model in small groups.

5. Connection with a Sacred Source: The compassion cultivation practices of Claremont School of Theology and Center for Engaged Compassion find their inspiration in all the wisdom traditions. *The Goddess Finishing School* curriculum is designed for a non-religious setting but respects the teachings of its predecessors

---

[11] Developed by the late American psychologist, Marshall B. Rosenberg, Nonviolent Communication, or NVC, is a nonviolent conflict resolution communications model which works to repair and restore relationships with an emphasis on the role of language, words, feelings and needs in resolving conflict.

and offers the space for participants to experience the D/divine in whatever manner is personally meaningful.

The Compassion Practice Curriculum

The Compassion Practice Curriculum is a twelve-week program of compassion-based contemplative practices that serves as compassion formation training for individuals to experience self-compassion, connect to their inner wisdom, and experience of the D/divine, as well as to extend compassion to others. *The Goddess Finishing School* curriculum, the focus of my research, is an adaptation of the twelve-week Compassion Practice curriculum to one six-hour curriculum for use with those who identify as girls and young women. The design and implementation draw heavily from and are inspired by the Compassion Practice and includes embodied-contemplative practices, as well as influences and resources from the social sciences.

There are so many pressures on today's youth, particularly on those who identify as girls and young women, that it is crucial that they have the tools and training necessary for their identity formation, and the development of agency and their capacities to be Self-led and in touch with their inner wisdom. The curriculum includes practices which support theoretical elements of agency: *intentionality, forethought, self-action,* and *self-reflection*. The inclusion of interpersonal neurobiology and social science findings lends the empirically based evidence needed to be accepted as a preventative and intervention program.[12] Because body image can be such a fraught area for those who identify as girls and young women, the intentional inclusion of embodied practices in the program offers participants the opportunity to re/connect with their body in adaptive ways. The session design is practice-focused, with minimal instruction or lecturing.

In the research and literature reviewed prior to my fieldwork, the recurring theme of youth's need to be *listened to* and *heard* is constant. It is crucial, too, for caring, consistent, and predictable adult presence. It is vital that youth feel confident that the adults

---

[12] See again the work of Bessel van der Kolk and Alane Daugherty, as well as *Under Pressure: Confronting the Epidemic of Stress and Anxiety in Girls* and *Untangled: Guiding Teenage Girls Through the Seven Transitions into Adulthood* by Lisa Damour.

tending to them can also *hear what they have to say when they have difficult things to say*—the adults have to be able to provide a grounded presence, a container that is stable and large enough to hold whatever the youth have need to deposit in it. The Compassion Practice can provide that grounding space—and can be taught not only to youth, but also to the caring adults who love them and care for them.

The Goddess Finishing School Curriculum

The curriculum was designed in order to answer the main queries of my research with a particular focus and intention on the following participant outcomes:

- To understand compassion/self-compassion—grounding, compassion for self and compassion for others
- To learn skills to:
- Understand the components of compassion (self, others, difficult others)
- Get grounded
- Develop a sense of awareness of embodiment (and embodied signs of dis-ease)
- To learn embodied practices to reduce/eliminate dis-ease
- To understand the movements of the Compassion Practice
- Practice compassion for self
- Practice compassion for others
- Practice compassion for difficult others
- Acknowledge and address the role stress plays in everyday life
- Identify Next Steps for making change in the community through compassionate engagement

As stated above, the design included, as one of the first activities of the program, the group's participatory development of a set of community guiding principles in order to define the conditions necessary to create safe (enough) space, build trust, and explicitly generate the agreed upon parameters for the program and its aftermath. We discussed the notion of *confidential enough*, with the group agreeing that, should they want to share about their experience of the program with persons who did not directly participate, they could do so, as long as the spoke from their own experience or about the practices they engaged with, and not about anyone else's experience. I then advised the participants to share only from their own experience as they felt comfortable, as well as an acknowledgement to the participants that difficult emotions might arise throughout or following the program, and should a participant experience difficulty processing their emotions, their teacher, the school's human development teacher, and the school counselor were available as additional resources.

My personal theology is relational—I believe in the interconnection immanent in all beings. This is a foundational orientation and starting place for any endeavor I engage in. Sharon Daloz Parks frames the need for relationality on a broader scale: "the importance of this relational perspective is heightened in a society and world in which growing numbers of neighborhoods feel threatened in some measure by intensified social diversity and the specter of random or organized violence. Because together we must create new, life-bearing realities, the potential contribution of this perspective cannot be overestimated."[13] In working with young people, I have found this orientation to be one that most resonates with the participants. I believe they can tell that I am invested in the process and in their flourishing as can be seen in their comments.

Reflection on the Contribution Participants' Voices

Throughout the *Goddess Finishing School* program, a primary intention was to make space for the voices of the participants. As experts on their own lived experience, the participants contributed the following advice to the experts of the academy so that we may learn from them:

1. The desire and need for programs such as *The Goddess Finishing School.*
2. The importance of being listened to and heard around their lived experience.
3. Have the experts gotten them wrong? The *Goddess Finishing School* participants expressed gratitude for the program, reporting they felt seen and heard. My sense is that the

---

[13] Sharon Daloz Parks, *Big Questions, Worthy Dreams: Mentoring Emerging Adults in Their Search for Meaning, Purpose, and Faith* (San Francisco, CA: Jossey-Bass, 2010), 59.

program provided a space for the participants to feel accepted and seen as who they are, not as projections. These findings are extant in the literature, but it's hard to live out. It is crucial for caring adults to resist, disrupt, and cease from perpetuating the disingenuous message often transmitted to youth regarding external pressure versus insinuating to youth that the pressures they feel are self-imposed. We must genuinely honor their agency and their role as co-contributors regarding their lived experience.

4. Participants' suggested changes: The participants reported that they appreciate the time and space for the program. They also want program to be flexible. They suggested a programmatic space where they can attend to whatever is relevant and generative for them in the moment–and they noted that the program needs to cover more than "friendships and periods," routinely discussed at school. The participants want adults to listen and offer safe space over time to engage these issues. The participants see a need for self-expression in this area and expressed the desire for this to be privileged.

The inclusion of the participants' voices aligns with the values and principles of Rogers' formulation of engaged-compassion practices described throughout, namely radical hospitality, self-compassion, a non-pathologizing, accepting stance toward interior movements, the role of story and personal narrative, and the invitation to welcome a sacred presence into one's midst. In alignment with my personal values and in accordance to the values and principles above, my research for the curriculum employed a transformative research and evaluation framework. *The Goddess Finishing School* curriculum development included input from the research participants themselves and one of their principal teachers. The principles of transformative paradigm research stress that "important ways of gathering insights under the transformative paradigm include methods of involving community members in the initial discussions of the research focus."[14] Indeed, one significant contribution of this study is the *inclusion* of the voices and opinions

---

[14] Donna M. Mertens, "Transformative Paradigm," *Journal of Mixed Methods Research* 1, no. 3 (2007): 214, https://doi.org/10.1177/1558689807302811.

of the people for whom the curriculum was developed. This study explicitly includes the voices and wisdom of the research participant community.

Essential Teaching Points of the Program

Returning to the idea of *being known as beloved*, and my longing as a young person to feel my value through the sense that at least *one person* took a dedicated interest in my wellbeing, *The Goddess Finishing School* proved to not only be a meaningful research project but also an experience of personal healing. It is from that vantage point of personal reflection and the researcher's data analysis that I have identified the following four teaching points of *The Goddess Finishing School* program as essential:

- It is vital for participants to understand that groundedness and compassion is at the heart of each person's natural state.
- Each person possesses and can connect to an internal voice and wisdom we can tap into.
- Stress is normal part of life, *and*
- There are tools and practices that exist to help us manage stress and regain calm.

Essential Programmatic Components

Drawing heavily from Rogers' and the Center for Engaged Compassion's principles of engaged-compassion programs, the design of *The Goddess Finishing School* curriculum was specifically crafted for its particular participants. I have identified the following as the essential programmatic components: intentional design and presentation of the content with minimal lecturing; radical hospitality; inclusion of embodied practices and different practices modalities; dedicated space and time for the program; and, perhaps most critically, providing a space for participants to experience being listened to and honored. While these components differ slightly from Rogers' Compassion Practice Curriculum, the differences are more in presentation than formulation.

The intentional design of the curriculum, specifically crafted for the particular participants, was the starting point for *The Goddess Finishing School*. I worked with one of the two main 6th grade teachers, envisioning the program. We met several times and

125

engaged in an ongoing collaboration crafting the program design for the participants. The buy-in of the boundary partners–the school administration and the participants' teacher was crucial to the program's success. The teacher's commitment to the study and her ability to prepare the participants for the program, such as screening the film, *Inside Out* (as an example of *parts*) and administering the pre and post surveys helped to make up for the fact that in order to deliver the pilot, I needed to condense program time significantly. While there can be standard elements to each iteration of the program, it is crucial to be intentional about each particular audience in the planning and design. The participant feedback and data showed that being introduced to content and given the opportunity to engage in actual practices and ways of thinking to acknowledge and manage stress, re/gain a sense of calm, tap into and hear one's inner voice all proved helpful. For many of the participants, this was the first time they encountered the practices offered in the program.

Another essential aspect of the intentional program design is the extension of deliberate radical hospitality–with love, care, and forethought going into crafting the space and the knowledge of the message of care this level of hospitality conveys to participants. Informal feedback from the Center for Engaged Compassion's programs always notes the important role hospitality plays in participants' experience of the program. Hospitality is not extra or an extravagance, it is an integral part of the curriculum of *The Goddess Finishing School* and indeed, a hallmark of all of Frank's work.

Dedicating a significant portion of the time allotted for the program on embodied practices enabled me to investigate a key supposition of my study: that embodied practices are an ideal "*way in*" to engaged compassion-based contemplative practices for this participant population. As such, I consider embodied practices a vital element of the program design. The findings from the data collected proved this supposition out – the embodied practices were consistently reported as among the most helpful. Additionally, the inclusion of different modalities of practices offers a variety of ways to reach participants where they are. This is a continuation of the Center for Engaged Compassion program's design, with additional attention to the modalities I thought would be most resonant with participants. The practices included embodied, creative, and imaginative writing and arts-based, guided practices, dialectic and relational practices, Non-violent Communication, role modeling of practices, and the movements of the Compassion Practice, such as PULSE and FLAG. It is important to think of youth participants as experts of their own lived experiences and learning styles, and to craft programs that are appropriate to a range of styles, rather than expecting participants to mold to the program design.

With regard to providing dedicated space and time to the program, a quote by the pastoral theologian, David Augsburger, comes to mind: "Being heard is so close to being loved that for the average person, they are almost indistinguishable."[15] Having an entire day devoted to the program validates that the program is important and demonstrates its significance by privileging precious instructional time to the program. Similarly, the time dedicated to the program helps to create the environment for participants to experience being listened to and honored. As with the Center for Engaged Compassion program, the *Goddess Finishing School* meets participants where they were, meaning everyone is welcome and the idea of *all is held* is modelled. Being listened to and heard is critical. As with the Augsburger quote above, the experience of authentically being listened to is seen as a gift. Regardless of the content covered, the impact of this grace of having that kind of space was reported as highly impactful for the participants.

Conclusion

The purpose of this chapter was to provide a description of the unique facets of Frank Rogers' formulation of engaged compassion-based practices. The chapter focuses on three primary areas: an overview of Rogers' formulation and practice of engaged compassion-based practices; the unique characteristics of Rogers' formulation of engaged compassion-based practices which position these practices as highly adaptable for any number of practical applications; and examples from *The Goddess Finishing School* program curriculum that are illustrative of the positive role these practices play in the spiritual/emotional/psycho-social development of female-identifying individuals–particularly with

---

[15] "David Augsburger Quotes," accessed March 23,2020, https://www.goodreads.com/author/quotes/388167.David_W_Augsburger.

respect to self-compassion, sense of self, agency, resilience, authenticity, relationality, and a sense of community.

The Goddess Finishing School curriculum is an adaptation of The Compassion Practice curriculum developed by Frank Rogers and colleagues at the Center for Engaged Compassion. *The Goddess Finishing School* pilot investigated the preventative and interventional use of compassion-based, embodied contemplative practices with those who identify as girls and young women and tested a curriculum which combines the approaches of engaged compassion, contemplative practices, physical embodiment, and interpersonal neurobiology with this population. The participants voiced their sense that, in their lives—at home and at school—they are under tremendous pressure to succeed, and that this pressure stems from internal and external stressors. Further, the participants expressed their desire to have "tools" and practices to re/gain a sense of calm and to manage and reduce stress. The program helped participants to surface and name the practices and ways that they already manage stress, but they discerned the need for additional effective tools. The curriculum offered new practices to the participants, which they felt would help them to reduce stress and regain/gain a sense of calm. Additionally, participants indicated their intention to continue to engage in these practices.

My hope for *The Goddess Finishing School* curriculum and pilot was to show that engagement with a compassion-based, embodied contemplative program can provide one significant way to support agency and identity formation, reduce stress, and empower those who identify as girls and young women. Indeed, a key finding of the program demonstrated that participants reported lower Perceived Stress Scale (PSS) scores, along with the acquisition of new skills and practices to re/gain a sense of calm and to manage and cope with stress. These intervention tools support the conditions and environment needed for positive development in the formation of identity, agency, authenticity, and empowerment.

The program adapted the organizing principles of Rogers' Compassion Practice Curriculum providing a structured program, while offering accessibility and flexibility for personalization. The participants were excited to be invited as thought partners into the program design, and they indicated their desire to have a similar program incorporated into their school curriculum with support from parents, school administrators, and teachers. Much of what I

128

discovered formally in the pilot validated and supported what I knew intuitively–that Rogers' curriculum and practices, from which I gained so much personally, could be modified to contribute to the flourishing and empowerment of those who identify as girls and young women. It is my hope to be to the young people I come in contact with, *that one caring adult* my young self so deeply yearned for, and that I was lucky enough to find in Frank Rogers, Jr.

Bibliography

Carter, Christopher. *The Spirit of Soul Food: Race, Faith, and Food Justice.* Urbana, IL: University of Illinois Press, 2021.

Damour, Lisa. *Untangled: Guiding Teenage Girls Through the Seven Transitions into Adulthood.* New York, NY: Ballantine Books, 2017.

Damour, Lisa. *Under Pressure: Confronting the Epidemic of Stress and Anxiety in Girls.* New York: Ballantine Books, 2019.

Daugherty, Alane. *The Power Within: From Neuroscience to Transformation.* Dubuque, IA: Kendall Hunt Publishing Co., 2008.

Daugherty, Alane. *From Mindfulness to Heartfulness: A Journey of Transformation Through the Science of Embodiment.* Bloomington, IN: Balboa Press, 2014.

Daugherty, Alane. *Unstressed: How Somatic Awareness Can Transform Your Body's Stress Response and Build Emotional Resilience.* New Harbinger Publications, Inc., 2019.

Dreitcer, Andrew. *Living Compassion: Loving like Jesus.* Nashville: Upper Room Books, 2017.

Holmes, Tom, Lauri Holmes, and Sharon Eckstein. *Parts Work: An Illustrated Guide to Your Inner Life.* Kalamazoo, MI: Winged Heart Press, 2007.

Mertens, Donna M. "Transformative Paradigm." *Journal of Mixed Methods Research* 1, no. 3 (2007): 212–214. https://doi.org/10.1177/1558689807302811.

Osmer, Richard. *Practical Theology: An Introduction.* Grand Rapids: Wm. B. Eerdmans Publishing Co., 2008.

Parks, Sharon Daloz. *Big Questions, Worthy Dreams: Mentoring Emerging Adults in Their Search for Meaning, Purpose and Faith.* San Francisco: Augsburg Fortress, 2011.

Rogers, Frank, Jr. *Practicing Compassion*. Nashville, TN: Upper Room, 2015.

Rogers, Frank Jr., Mark Yaconelli, and Andy Dreitcer. *The Way of Radical Compassion: Following the Spiritual Path of Jesus*. Claremont, CA: Center for Engaged Compassion, 2015.

Rosenberg, Marshall B. *Nonviolent Communication: A Language of Life*. Seoul: KNVC, 2011.

Schwartz, Richard C. "Don't Look Back." *Family Therapy Networker*. (March/April 1997): 7-12.

Schwartz, Richard C. *Introduction to The Internal Family Systems Model*. Oak Park, IL: Trailheads Publications, 2001.

Schwartz, Richard C. "The Larger Self." *Psychotherapy Networker* 8, no. 3 (May/June 2004).

Van der Kolk, Bessel. *The Body Keeps the Score*. New York: Penguin, 2014.

Frank Rogers, Jr. "As Spiritual Teacher, Mentor, and Friend"

Nancy Fowler

Simply put, my life has been transformed because of Frank Rogers, Jr. It began in my first class with him, Religious Education, in the fall of 2001. Frank's impact was greatly enhanced when he became my Ph.D. advisor in 2012. His inspiration helped to carry me through some intense challenges and tragedy in my family, and continues today. Following are some of the details of my experiences with Frank, including some personal stories to demonstrate specifically how I have been transformed through Frank's guidance and mentorship as he practiced the Compassion Practice himself.

Frank Rogers is an awesome storyteller. He weaves stories throughout his writings, teaching, and presentations. These stories are critical to helping one to understand the concepts that have been created by Frank in his Compassion Practice. I often retell some of Frank's stories when I am discussing the Practice with anyone unfamiliar with it. I consider it an honor and privilege to mimic Frank by weaving in my own stories here to illustrate what the Compassion Practice has done for me, how it has transformed me and helped me through intense life challenges. If you are unfamiliar with the Compassion Practice, it might be helpful to first review the program in the appendix prior to reading the following stories of my insights and transformations that I received through the Internal Family Systems model of therapy (IFS) and the Compassion Practice.

Early Experience with Frank Rogers

I first met Frank early in my M.Div. program at CST, in his course on Religious Education. Because of extreme traffic, I was about 15 minutes late for the first class meeting – the only class to which I was late my entire tenure at CST. Because Frank knows that learning can happen more effectively in smaller groups, Frank had already formed groups before my arrival. When I entered, I quickly

131

sat down in the closest chair. This established my group for the semester. They immediately said, "Quick, write down a dream of yours." If I had more time, I might have come up with something different, but I wrote down the first thing that came to my mind: "Go to the Holy Land." I am not even sure where that came from, I had not known it as a deep desire. But there it was. We were then invited to discuss our dreams within the small group, so I had to consider why I would want to go there. I knew there was a draw because that was where Jesus had lived. I also knew there was a conflict, but I knew little of any details. What this did do was open me up to an extraordinary experience in that class. The second class meeting was September 13, 2001. Yes, two days after 9/11. I think that class session was just what each of us needed. Through his words and actions, Frank provided a space for us to do what we needed in that moment, including: processing what had happened, considering any actions we might take, quiet reflection, prayer, etc. I will never forget the closing circle for that day. I do not remember Frank's specific words, but I do know that there was not a dry eye in the room. Choosing the Holy Land as my dream became quite timely at that moment. I spent the rest of the semester focusing on Israel-Palestine through scripture and researching the issues. This connection to Israel-Palestine led to a deeper relationship with Frank a decade later.

Pursuing a Ph.D.

My denomination is the Christian Church (Disciples of Christ), so I was able to connect with the Disciples Seminary Foundation (DSF), just across the street from CST. The dean in 2001, Rod Parrott, had been taking groups on tours of Israel-Palestine designed to learn more about the situation, as well as visit Holy Sites. I asked him to put me on the list for the next trip. There were no trips for several years because of the violent second intifada, and because Rod retired. The new dean, Tamara Nichols Rodenberg, organized a trip that I joined in 2008, soon after my graduation from CST with my M.Div. That trip was a life-transforming experience. When we asked Palestinians what they wanted from us, they said, "Tell our story." I came home, prepared a presentation, and went to a number of churches in Southern California to tell their story. Two years later, sensing that I was called to do more, I led a similar, peace-building

132

trip to Palestine with the help of Cathy Nichols, a former Global Ministries (a partner ministry with the United Church of Christ) mission co-worker to Sabeel in Jerusalem. She organized the itinerary and traveled with us. This prepared me to lead trips on my own, and I led four more.

On that first DSF-led trip, we had a tour chaplain travel with us, Jeff Wright, who with his wife, led annual tours of Israel-Palestine. It happened that Frank Rogers was on one of those tours just as I was beginning to feel stirrings to continue my education focusing on spirituality and mission. Through the current dean of DSF, Mark Parsons, who knew of my Palestine connection, I discovered that Frank had just returned from that trip, and that he came back wanting to do something with spirituality and peace for Palestine. He had begun offering degree programs in spiritual formation. With that knowledge, and my previous experience with Frank, I entered into to the Ph.D. program, with Frank as my advisor and doctoral mentor. My intent was to focus on Palestine for my dissertation.

I began taking courses in Fall 2012, with my first class taught by Frank. He again formed small groups in the class. I remember some deep, rich discussions within my group. His first book on the Compassion Practice, *Practicing Compassion*, was not published until 2015, but the practice was already well developed, and compassion, and the concepts of the practice, were at the heart of his teachings. One of the books for the class was by Jay Earley, *Self-Therapy: A Step-by-Step Guide to Creating Wholeness and Healing Your Inner Child Using IFS, A New, Cutting-Edge Psychotherapy*. The principles of the Internal Family Systems model of therapy (IFS) are incorporated into the self-compassion step of the Compassion Practice. From the beginning, I was captivated by Earley's book, and Frank's presentations. This was my first IFS revelation, and its importance for me personally:

When I was working toward my Masters of Divinity degree at CST, our pastoral care and counseling professor recommended that all ministers should work with a therapist. Because we will be providing pastoral care for others, we need to discover, and heal, our own issues as much as possible. Otherwise, we might be surprised when a problem of a parishioner sparks an emotional response in ourselves that inhibits our ability to serve others well. I remember talking with my therapist about my father; I had never felt that I could ever be good enough for him. My therapist focused in on my Little Girl inside. I resented this. When she asked me to imagine sitting on a swing with my Little Girl, I became angry. That's MY Little Girl! How dare you tell me what to do with her! I left that therapist, without even telling her I would not be back. Why did I get angry when she told me what to do with her – so angry that I never returned?

It was in that first foray into IFS that I met and spent time with my Little Girl. I first met "Switch," my protector that would distract my mind whenever he sensed I was getting too close to this exile; his fear was that I would be overwhelmed by this Little Girl who believed that she would/could never be good enough. I now understand that my protector made me angry at my therapist in order to keep me away from my Little Girl. She was five or six years old, wearing drab hand-me-downs (I was the third daughter), and she was looking sad and dejected. I let her know how old I am and all that I have accomplished. It was not long, a few sessions with her, before I saw a real transformation in her. She now wears a fancy white dress and a big smile. And she dances! She knows that she is good enough. I now know that I am good enough, too.[1]

I continued a full-time schedule of courses, including any course that was offered by Frank, and any course that might include the principles of Compassion Practice and IFS. One of these courses, Embodied Spirituality, was taught by Frank's wife, Dr. Alane Daugherty, a neurophysiologist and Cal Poly Pomona professor. Frank would occasionally enhance his own courses by bringing in Alane. For the school year, 2013/2014, I enrolled in Frank Rogers' Compassion Practice retreat-centered course. There were four long-weekend retreats, with weekly zoom meetings in between. These were co-led by Alane and two of Frank's colleagues, Nancy Linton and Doug Frank. I was hooked! The most profound meditation experience in that first Compassion Practice course centered on this ordination experience:

When I began to feel called to seminary, I was surprised, especially when others began to tell me I should be a minister. I did not feel worthy and I did not want to be a minister. I gradually began

---

[1] Jay Earley, *Self-Therapy: A Step-by-Step Guide to Creating Wholeness and Healing Your Inner Child Using IFS, A New, Cutting-Edge Psychotherapy* (Minneapolis: Mill City Press, 2009).

to tell people about my sense of call, probably hoping that someone would set me straight. Well, I guess that did happen. Everyone encouraged me to go. Even the Jewish director of my kids' preschool told me I should be a minister. So I applied to CST and was accepted. Living in San Diego with two young children (kindergarten and second grade), and not knowing why I was there, I began by taking one course at a time. I gradually took more courses, but it took me eight years to complete my degree.

The natural process was to then be ordained. Our regional minister, Don Shelton, was retiring and, if I had to do this, I wanted him to be the one to officiate my ordination. So I set the date. This is when I really began to feel hesitance, to the point that I found it difficult to plan my program. Friends stepped up to help in a variety of ways, one even helping to help set up my program. When Maria Tafoya told me that the laying on of hands in her ordination was a highlight of her life, I decided that I could do it for that. Little did I suspect that this act would be the most challenging part of the ordination. At the moment that Rev. Shelton placed his hand on my head, I heard a voice that was so loud that I thought everyone must have heard it, "I'm a fraud!" What? What does that mean? I completed seminary – with good grades. I was approved for ordination by the Committee on Ministry? These thoughts continued in the years following my ordination.

Six years after my ordination, I was participating in a two semester, retreat-centered CST course in the Compassion Practice, taught by Frank Rogers. There were several long weekends at a retreat center, and there were weekly Zoom gatherings in between. The retreat program consisted of plenary sessions with teaching and meditations, small group gatherings of six to eight with a facilitator, and individual time for meditating and processing. During the third retreat, we were sent out on our own to meditate on a particularly challenging part. When I said I did not have one in mind, I was asked by my small group facilitator, Doug Frank, "Have you ever heard a voice?" YES! Referring to a handout, I was guided to work with my parts. Suddenly, up popped a middle-school aged girl wearing a full-sized, man's brown suit. And then I understood. I was raised in a patriarchal home – I could never be good enough since I was not male. And I was taken to a patriarchal church. Women were to be silent in church, never to teach a man. Certainly, as a woman, I could never be ordained. I was a fraud to present myself to be ordained.

The next words I saw on our handout were *imago dei*, the image of God. I, a woman, was created in the image of God. We were due back in our small groups to share our meditation experiences, but I needed to do something first. I went outside, raised my arms out wide, spun around, and said "I am a woman! I am made in the image of God! I am good enough! I am not a fraud!"

As I continued with my courses, I began to consider how I might incorporate my desire to bring hope to Palestine with the Compassion Practice. With input from Mitri Raheb, then pastor of Christmas Lutheran Church in Bethlehem, and Belva Brown Jordan, then dean of DSF, and with Frank's approval, I decided to create a program using the Compassion Practice to bring conversation about Israel-Palestine into Christian congregations. I would use a listening tool introduced to me by Frank, the Public Conversation Project (now Essential Partners), to help dialog participants to be open to listening to truth rather than reacting based on previous beliefs and emotion.

I completed my courses and began to study for my qualifying exams. Throughout this time, I took every opportunity to participate in Compassion Practice experiences, through courses, small groups, and personal time. I was very often surprised at what would be revealed during the meditations. I was discovering more about who I am, and why I react to situations in the ways that I do. Following is an example of this:

I have learned through Compassion Practice and IFS that if I get more emotional – maybe angry or sad – than is really warranted, there is probably a wounded part underneath that needs tending. A number of years ago I had volunteered to help lead a women's spiritual day-retreat. However, I got a call from my mother early in the week asking me to go with her to a funeral on that Saturday. The father of the family that lived across the street from my childhood home had died. Of course I would go with my mom to the service! The next day I had an opportunity to meet with several women of our retreat group, including the chair. When I told her that I couldn't make it Saturday so I could attend the funeral of a family friend, she shot back at me, "You have to come to our meeting to bring what you promised!" I was stunned. I was even more stunned when I immediately began to cry. I had to walk away to try to pull myself together. When I went back to her, I had barely started in about Saturday when she again shot back at me. "We are counting on you. You have a responsibility." And again, I was stunned and began to cry. A good friend witnessed this and volunteered to take my spot so I could attend the service. But the point is, what happened? Why was I so activated? For years, I blamed her. She had hurt me deeply while I had thought she was my friend. It wasn't until years later when I started working with the Compassion Practice that I began to look at this differently. Yes, I had been hurt when she seemed to be so uncaring, but that shouldn't have sparked my intense reaction. As I began to look inside, I realized that the deep emotional response was related to my relationship with the daughter of the man who died. From fifth grade through high school, she bounced between being my best friend and someone who could be pretty cruel. Thinking about it, I would call her a bully. But she lived across the street and we carpooled to school so I had to be with her. Hearing about the death of her father had re-exposed all the hidden pain from that relationship. That's what was hurting so badly. That's why I was so easily brought to tears.

Unexpected Life Events

Sadly, while I was working on my Ph.D. program, and on my mental/emotional/spiritual health, my son Nick was heading down a dark path. He was gay and the bullying started when he was in kindergarten. When, at five-years-old, he told me he did not want to be alive, we discovered that he had some serious mental health challenges. This began a lifetime of therapy for depression and anxiety. He found "self-medication" in eighth grade, something he never could get past. He had contemplated, and even tried, suicide; we first knew of this when he was 21. This was the cause of deep fear, and intense emotions. I knew my work with Compassion Practice was helping me to be calmer. Following is an experience with Nick when I knew how much I was transformed by the practice:

We tried so many different ways to help Nick to move forward. After time in rehab and transitional living, we let him rent a studio apartment. Sadly, that only lasted a few months. After a visit with him, a friend of his followed me back out to my car to let me know how much Nick was using. He said that Nick – much loved, popular

137

Nick – was losing friends because of it. Some because they could not let themselves be caught up in the use. Some because they did not want to watch him die. A few days later, that same friend helped us with an intervention to take him out of his apartment and into detox. His sober guide and mentor, Brian, was also with us. I was openly emotional with mixed sadness and anger. We finally got him into the car and we delivered an angry young man into what we hoped would be life-saving detox. We let him know that it would be a week before we came to get him.

During that week, I attended the third of a series of four Compassion Practice retreats. We were back to get Nick two days after that and we informed him that we were going to take him directly to rehab. This did not go over well! He went storming around the facility, even spitting on a picture on the wall. Then he came up to challenge me. He said, "Mom! Look me in the eye! If you make me do this, I will resent you for a very long time!" I very calmly responded, "Nick, if that's what it takes for you to be healthy, I'm willing to risk that." He walked away. I was then told that he was telling others that he was going to just walk out of the rehab after we put him in there. I went to him and asked if he was going to leave the rehab after we left. He said, "I might." I calmly said, "If you're planning to leave, why don't we just put all of your things out in the front yard here?" Again, he walked away. When we went to get in our car, he came with us and went into the rehab.

Nick's sober companion, Brian Stark, was with us and observed all of the interactions between Nick and me. He worried about me because he knew how upset I could get over Nick. He shared later that he was shocked that I had remained completely calm over the types of interactions with Nick that had previously sparked intense sadness and/or anger. I knew that I had remained calm – I was truly calm, not just stuffing my emotions down to get through the moment – because of my work with the Compassion Practice, especially just coming off of an intense weekend with it. Brian told me he wanted that, too, and he did participate in a later Compassion Practice retreat series.

In spite of all of our efforts, on July 4, 2015, Nick died by suicide. At 24, he just could not handle the pain of his life anymore and succeeded in ending his sad life. Nick's death challenged every part of me. However, Frank gave me a most needed gift right before he died:

The single most significant impact on my life was the direct result of a retreat led by Frank. This was a week-long retreat held on a small college campus in Oregon. The site was along a logging road, and was surrounded by forest. Housing was in cabins; I shared with one other woman who had to leave after a few days because she had not been able to attain childcare for the full week. The facilities included a main hall for dining and plenary sessions, and a chapel set back into the forest. The sessions incorporated training and practice of IFS and the Compassion Practice, spiritual direction, prayer and worship, and silent mornings.

For me, the retreat began with a bang. I had gone with an open mind, knowing that whatever happened there would be helpful for me. After all, this was organized and led by Frank Rogers. Before our first gathering, I went into the bathroom off of the hall. There on a shelf sat a container of Boraxo soap. My father retired from US Borax after twenty-eight years of employment. My immediate thought was, "Okay. This retreat is about my dad." And it was! Certainly, there were times when I opened to other invitations to seek healing and wholeness within, but it would very often revert to work on my dad.

About mid-week, during a spiritual direction session (using IFS) with Nancy Linton, I felt an overwhelming sense of a lack of any love or approval from my father. I suddenly felt my dad's presence with me. At the end of our session, Nancy encouraged me, if I felt his presence again, to give back to him whatever I had found loveless or oppressive. That was truly a gift!

That same evening, after the conclusion of the day's sessions, I returned to my cabin, where I would be alone since my roommate had gone home. Once again, I sensed the presence of my father. Following Nancy's advice, I began to tell my dad what I had felt from his actions, while growing up, and even as an adult. I do not even remember everything I said to him, but it was quite a litany. Each comment was essentially, "When you …, it was not okay." I know that the first one was, "When you tickled me until I cried, it was not okay." I had initially sensed anger toward me for the despairing things I had been saying, and thinking, about him throughout the retreat. As I continued on, I sensed a shrinking of his presence, as if he were slumping under the condemnations. I then followed with another of Nancy's suggestions. I told him that he did not need to keep all that had just been put on him. He did not need to carry all of this on his own. He could pass what had been oppressive to him to whomever was appropriate. I certainly do not know everything that was difficult for him, but I do know some. When he was twelve, he was delivering magazines on his route when he was hit by a truck. He knew he was hurt, but he knew he would be in trouble with his parents if he did not finish his route. When he got home, he told them what happened, but they did nothing, including take him to the doctor. He suffered with a bad back his whole life. Much later, his back got so painful that he went to the doctor for it. X-rays showed that he had a vertebra that had been previously broken. He could pass that pain, both physical and emotional, and anything else that had hurt him (like the extreme favoritism by his mother for his sister), back to his parents. I then sensed a conclusion to this time with him. I have not felt his presence in any strong way since, but this episode seemingly opened a next path for me.

My next experience at the retreat was a sensing of the never loved or approved of Exile. It seems that my protector parts finally recognized that I could discover this part and not be overwhelmed. She first appeared deep in an alcove, looking afraid. I did not know how to coax her out, and she seemed to be afraid even of me. Did she not trust me? I guess I could not blame her. Finally, through a spiritual direction (using IFS) with Frank, she began to emerge. However, apparently still not trusting me, she went to sit on Mary's lap. I have felt a deep connection to Mary because we have both had to live with the tragedy of a death of a child, so this made sense to me. And I knew she was comforted and safe, and loved!

I returned from the retreat feeling more whole spiritually, emotionally, and mentally than maybe any time in my life. I looked forward to basking in, and building on, these feelings. However, less than 24 hours after I returned home, we got the word that Nick had overdosed and died. Because of the retreat, which built on all of my previous Compassion Practice and IFS experience, I was in the best possible state to deal with everything around his death, including: announcing it, what to do with his body, his services, and just plain missing the hell out of him. In addition, I continued to benefit from the practice and IFS, as shown here:

Sometime in the first few months after Nick died, I was feeling very heavy with sadness. It was like there was a heavy weight of sadness pressing down on me. I sensed that there was something more to this; it wasn't my "usual" level of grief and sadness. So I decided to go inside to see if I could learn more about this. As I began to quiet my mind, it didn't take long before I heard a voice inside, "I would have held you." Immediately, the tears came because I knew who this was. This was the sad mom part of me who would never have let Nick die alone. I began to talk to her, "Really? You would have held him, knowing what he was going to do?" By this time, I was sobbing. And then I heard, "If he was going to do it no matter what, I would have held him." Yes! I get that! And with that, I felt the weight of sadness lighten. I haven't felt that same heaviness since.

I had twice participated in the retreat-centered program of the Compassion Practice, once for course credit, and once for training to be a Compassion Practice facilitator. About six months after Nick died, I chose to again participate in the retreat. One of the main qualities of the practice is the contemplative nature. Every step includes meditations. It is during these meditations that receive incredible gifts, from essential grounding to discovering hidden parts. Sometimes my heart takes me to a place that is not related to what is being guided. That was exactly what I needed:

It was at a Compassion Retreat six months after Nick died that I had my first vision of him. We had entered into a guided meditation, having been invited to breathe deeply and rhythmically. When we were then invited to go into our sacred space, I looked toward my internal room. There was a window and a door, where I had never seen either before; I had previously just found myself inside. When I looked through the open window, there was Nick. Then suddenly, several parts blocked my way, telling me that it was too dangerous to go in. I would be overwhelmed with sadness. I turned to them and said that I thought I would be okay. I told them that they could watch through the window to make sure that I did not need to step in to protect me. I then asked them to sit down and wait on the nearby bench. They sat down.

When I went to the door, Nick said to me, "Come on in, Mom. I want to take care of you the way you took care of me." When I walked in, he said, "I am so happy here." As we were being guided back from the meditation, Nick went to the door and said to my waiting parts, "I will never hurt her again."

Frank acknowledges that we may not always follow the guidance in a meditation. He says, "Your soul knows what you need." My soul needed to see Nick.

Grief

Certainly, the shock of grief was intense. I knew that I wanted to continue my Ph.D. program, but I found that I could not carry the pain of the plight of the Palestinians with the pain of my grief. I had to let Palestine go, at least in the intense work of a dissertation. Because Nick's mental illness led to his death, I decided to focus on mental health for my dissertation. Sadly, conversation about mental health in churches has typically ranged from misinformed to non-existent. The program I had envisioned for Palestine conversations seemed to fit well with taking mental health conversations into churches. I even did a trial run that produced some promising results. However, my knowledge and understanding of mental health was lacking. I had never personally experienced clinical depression or anxiety. I was doing a lot of reading to learn what I could. In the middle of that, I became overcome with my focus on grief, and I knew that this was to become the focus of my dissertation. It took one meeting with Frank to not only gain approval for this change, but also to receive critical guidance for the path forward. I know Frank had looked forward to pursuing a project that could contribute to a hope for peace for Palestine, but he never showed anything but full support for the new direction for my project.

The guidance received in that meeting was to create an event focused on grief as a basis for a dissertation study. The design of such a workshop had been so well patterned by Frank. Having previously attended Compassion Practice trainings and workshops, including those that used the practice to focus on a particular issue, I knew that it could be effectively focused on grief for the dissertation study. The event I created was a one-day workshop using the Compassion Practice as a way to process grief. The ten participants had all lost at least one child. The deaths ranged from miscarriage, to perinatal death, to older children who died from natural causes or suicide. I used my own stories and experiences to weave through the presentation, modeled after Frank's effective use of storytelling to illustrate the teachings, often sharing his own very personal experiences. The surveys following the workshop demonstrated that this event did offer relief, and even healing, to the participants. This truly demonstrates the versatility of the Compassion Practice, that it can even be used to help relieve some of the pain of losing a child. My research for my dissertation showed that the worst loss is the death of a child. We who are having to go forward after such a loss need such support. I loved being able to share with others what had provided me so much compassionate care as I have moved forward through my own grief. This sense of fulfillment has guided me through completion of my degree and beyond.

Ministering Forward

The Internal Family Systems model of therapy course at CST, taught by Dr. Rogers, benefited me greatly. In addition to providing healing experiences on its own, it also helped me to better understand the self-compassion piece of the Compassion Practice. I wanted more IFS so when I learned that I could participate in a deeper IFS training, I jumped at the chance. Over a year's time and six intensive three-day sessions, I received the same IFS training that a therapist must get to be qualified to be an IFS Therapist. I am not a therapist; I am now an IFS Practitioner. Throughout the training, we used IFS therapy on ourselves in ways that helped us to better understand the program. I had some amazingly beneficial, even healing experiences in the process. I believe that this training helps me to be a better Compassion Practice facilitator.

It had been suggested by a few respected others that I might serve well as a spiritual director. Dr. Rogers is a spiritual director, using IFS, and that interested me very much. When he offered the opportunity to earn certification as such a spiritual director, through Stillpoint: The Center for Christian Spirituality,[2] I was excited. I am now a certified spiritual director, using IFS.

As I have indicated, I want to share with others all that has been so helpful to me. The additional training presented in the previous section has certainly served me well through my difficult times, and it has also given me much that can help me to serve others through their challenges and tragedies. I now seek ways to do that. One

---

[2] Stillpoint: The Center for Christian Spirituality, https://stillpointca.org/

143

major project that will serve this purpose is a book that I am writing on my experiences of loss and compassionate care. Following are other prospects that I continue to cultivate for this purpose.

BeLOVEd, started by Rev. J. "Dale" Suggs, is a progressive, inclusive, and contemplative Christian Community of the Christian Church (Disciples of Christ). Dale's wife Shelly was then a student of spiritual formation at CST, where she was introduced to Frank Rogers and his Compassion Practice. Almost from their inception eight years ago, BeLOVEd has incorporated the Compassion Practice into their overall format, including it in worship services and gatherings. They have now created a non-profit, the BeLOVEd Compassion Network (BCN), offering a variety of compassion-based trainings and gatherings. They have offered my greatest opportunity for personal growth through my participation with them in the Compassion Practice, in sharing in the group experiences and in helping to facilitate the practice. I have had numerous opportunities to facilitate the Compassion Practice, and to present special trainings, including IFS. Their greatest gift for me was their help and support for the workshop on grief following the death of a child(ren) for my dissertation, by providing the site and catering for the day-long workshop, as well as being present to assist in any way needed. I continue to participate in Compassion Practice groups and now serve on the BCN board of directors.

BeLOVEd sponsored a second grief workshop for me to lead. This one was not focused on the death of a child; any form of grief was included. One participant lost his wife two years prior. One lost his father, not to death, but to ultra conservative Christianity; he was no longer accepted by his father. One of the participants had participated in the dissertation workshop. Two of her children had died, one by suicide. She joined this workshop because the first one had helped her and she now needed help because her husband had since died. One had lost her son to suicide seven years prior. I soon after received a note from her that read, "You fed my soul." I could not ask to do more than that.

In addition to group settings, I feel fulfilled through one-on-one interactions with others who are dealing with challenges. This can even happen in a phone conversation(s) with someone whom I have never met. My training and experience with the Compassion Practice, IFS, and spiritual direction, and my own journey through challenges and tragedy, have prepared me to be fully present and to

144

listen to the needs presented. Plus, my level of compassion has been enhanced by my loss and by the development of a compassionate presence through my ten years with the Compassion Practice.

My IFS therapist calls this work my sealed orders. I had never heard that term before. I found a good description of this in *Sleeping with Bread: Holding What Gives You Life*, suggested reading for a Frank Rogers course. It's like you have a conversation with God before you were born about your purpose in the world. Then you spend your life trying to discover what that purpose is.[3] That makes total sense to me. Outside of being a mother, when I am leading a workshop, or guiding an individual in a caring conversation, I feel more fulfilled than at any time in my life.

Conclusion

I have suffered a loss that my studies in grief described as the most difficult, the death of a child. The most challenging death is suicide. I had to face both when Nick died.

Frank Rogers' Compassion Practice, and his truly compassionate presence, have contributed so greatly to my ability to go forward. This has been enhanced by what I believe is the discovery of employing these gifts for my true purpose, my sealed orders.

Thank you, Frank!

Bibliography

Earley, Jay. *Self-Therapy: A Step-by-Step Guide to Creating Wholeness and Healing Your Inner Child Using IFS, A New, Cutting-Edge Psychotherapy*. Minneapolis: Mill City Press, 2009.

Linn, Dennis, Sheila Fabricant Linn, and Matthew Linn. *Sleeping with Bread: Holding What Gives You Life*. Mahwah, New Jersey: Paulist Press, 1995, 20-21.

Stillpoint: The Center for Christian Spirituality, https://stillpointca.org/.

Rogers, Frank, Jr. *Compassion in Practice: The Way of Jesus*. Nashville: Upper Room Books, 2016.

---

[3] Dennis Linn, Sheila Fabricant Linn, and Matthew Linn, *Sleeping with Bread: Holding What Gives You Life* (Mahwah, New Jersey: Paulist Press, 1995), 20-21.

Rogers, Frank, Jr. *Practicing Compassion.* Nashville: Upper Room Books, 2015.

Rogers, Frank, Jr. Mark Yaconelli, and Andy Dreitcer, *The Way of Radical Compassion: Following the Spiritual Path of Jesus.* Claremont, CA: The Center for Engaged Compassion, 2015.

Frank's Journey, Emotional Healing, and The Compassion Practice: A Scientific Perspective

Alane Daughtery

Kendra's grandmother was suffering. She had been diagnosed with stage four cancer, and in addition to the physical pain it caused, she was experiencing a great deal of emotional distress. She was bearing her fear of cancer and resurfacing grief over losing her husband several years earlier; she yearned for Kendra to be by her side. She and Kendra were exceptionally close; she needed Kendra's support and someone to come in and cook dinner for her a few evenings a week when the visiting nurse could not be there. Most of all, she wanted the companionship of her closest loved one as she made this final journey of her life. Kendra longed to be there for her grandmother; Kendra sincerely loved her and had the time and availability to help. She deeply ached to feel genuine compassion for her grandmother and knew if she could, a deep and loving connection would ensue, a priceless gift knowing her grandmother's time was limited. Instead, despite how hard Kendra tried, she found herself resistant, angry, and defensive. Kendra hated herself for not being able to feel compassionate or emotionally available to this woman she loved, but something was blocking her ability to do so. She was numb, scared, and entangled in her reactivity, for Kendra had her own story.

Her past was influencing Kendra's present, and she was largely unaware. Her history included life experiences that colored her perceptions and inhibited her ability to behave as she desired. Her grandmother also had a life narrative of challenging life events that prevented her from being fully grounded in the present. As a result, Kendra and her grandmother had diminished emotional capacities to navigate the current trials they were facing. They needed to rescript some of their built-in emotional programs before they could approach what was to come with love, compassion, and entire presence.

As you will see through this chapter, ultimately, Kendra's story is one of deep healing. The healing was regenerative, allowing her to be there for her grandmother in her final days. But, also, and

147

importantly, it allowed her to be there for herself. Through a step-by-step process of inner work, she could cultivate transformative compassion for herself. From there, she could extend sincere love, kindness, and understanding to her grandmother, the type of compassion her grandmother longed for in this leg of her life's journey.

Frank's Journey

Frank Rogers, Jr. knows this type of compassion. For him, developing compassion for self and others is a process of deep inner work. He does this work himself, teaches, and leads others in it. I can attest to the regenerative power of this inner process; I have seen it in him and others he has led down this same path. Further, I can provide a scientific framework of how this healing happens, perhaps offering a tangible explanation of the transformative experience that many find hard to articulate. The purpose of this chapter is to briefly describe Frank's healing journey and how he came to develop the Compassion Practice - the focus of his current vocation. Finally, it provides a theoretical understanding of the science supporting his work. My distinct vantage point allows me to speak about these areas.

You see, Frank Rogers is my beloved, my best friend, and my colleague. As such, I have the cherished and unique opportunity to gaze upon him and his work through different colored lenses. Although the emphasis of Frank's work has shifted over the years, his most recent work has been on the development of compassion for self and others, and it is through this context that I write. Frank believes, as do I, that the development of compassion is one of the few authentic healing sources in our world.

Frank does this work himself, and he knows trauma. That trauma took him on an all-consuming journey of inner healing that eventually evolved into the Compassion Practice.

Many of us can only imagine the extent of childhood adversity Frank endured. Those that can relate may know the depths of despair he experienced and the far-reaching effects of that trauma in every nook and cranny of his life. No matter how hard one tries to escape or suppress the trauma, it resurfaces with a vengeance. For Frank, it was all-consuming and, among other things, led to

148

significant memory lapses, recurring nightmares, and mental institution stays under suicide watch.

Frank also knows how to heal – the 'know it in your bones' type of personal restoration where there is no doubt deep transformation has occurred. How did he come to know this? First, he was committed to finding his way to stable and thriving emotional health. Then, through steadfast resolution, trial, and error, he developed a process of inner work best described as a roadmap to personal healing. At its foundation is the belief that every internal hardship is a whimper (or scream) for personal restoration from some past emotional trauma. These experiences can range along the continuum from 'micro-traumas' that many of us experience in the process of life to more considerable emotional and mental traumas caused by significant life events. Regardless, they are our past life experiences buried deep in our psyche that cause current emotional pain and skewed perceptions when triggered. Further, these internal movements long for restoration and balance, and the best way we can facilitate this is to hold them in a state of self-compassion.

An additional and meaningful realization came with the awareness that others are wired with these internal movements. Thus, it is easier to have compassion for them as well. Frank's personal journey now also became his vocational journey.

The Compassion Practice is Born

A significant shift in Frank's work came when he described his healing process to two close friends and colleagues, Andrew Drietcer and Mark Yaconelli. They helped to articulate the strategy in a step-by-step format and give it a name – thus, the Compassion Practice was born. Although it is not my intention here to provide specifics on the Compassion Practice, generally speaking, it was Frank's process of healing crafted into an accessible format and formulated for the development of self-compassion and compassion for others.

It was in this context that we came to know each other. Frank's colleague Andrew was putting on a conference on spirituality and neuroscience, which I attended as I had just finished writing a book on the topic. A mutual friend gave Andy a copy of my book, and after reading it, Andy wanted Frank to meet me. To hear Frank tell

149

it, Andy explained, "She can provide the science of why what we do works." I will share that science shortly, but first, I share what I observed once they gave the Compassion Practice a name, a designated process, and a forum for sharing it with others desiring emotional regeneration. It was here I witnessed his work in action.

I often co-led retreats with him centered around the Compassion Practice, and here I viewed what can only be described as profound personal transformation in many retreatants. I also had the opportunity to do guest lectures in his classes at The Claremont School of Theology. In these courses, the students learned the Compassion Practice from both an experiential and didactic point of view, and I was fortunate to have conversations around both. One thing was apparent in all the environments I was observing the Compassion Practice in action: a significant and positive internal shift was occurring, and it was often hard to articulate. Nevertheless, there was an abundance of stories, stories like Kendra's, where something so significant was happening that it was helpful for some to have a framework of understanding. This framework of understanding is my contribution to Frank's work here.

The work that Frank and I do is different yet synergistic. Again, it is not my purpose to lay out the fundamentals of the Compassion Practice. Frank has done that in his other work[1].My goal is to provide a basic scientific understanding of the type of healing that occurs through its use and that of similar practices. He has also influenced my work; thus, I have had the pleasure of facilitating journeys such as Kendra's. Although Kendra did not specifically engage in the Compassion Practice, her process of inner work was similar enough to draw the same conclusions.

I don't claim to speak for Frank in the discourse that follows. We are colleagues in overlapping yet different fields; our interpretations may vary slightly, although fundamentally are the same. From a scientific standpoint, the following discourse is my take on the healing potential of his work, similar work, and work that he has influenced.

---

[1] See Frank Rogers, *Practicing Compassion* (Nashville, TN: Fresh Air Books, 2015) and Frank Rogers, *Compassion in Practice: The Way of Jesus* (Nashville, TN: Upper Room Books, 2016)

The Importance of the Implicit

Understanding the concepts of implicit memory and memory reconsolidation is helpful to fully grasp the transformative potential of techniques such as the Compassion Practice. I will elaborate on these concepts below and ultimately entertain their part in emotional revitalization in general and the Compassion Practice in particular.

Implicit memory is the process by which all our past life experiences are encoded deep in the neural nets of our emotional brain and used as a mechanism to provide an appraisal of all future events. Sometimes the meaning ascribed is accurate, and sometimes, it is darkly colored by the nature of the initial event(s)[2].

We are all profoundly influenced by implicit memory, and most of us are unaware of the extent of its impact. All our emotional perceptions, reactions, behaviors, and choices are under its influence. Even the term implicit memory is confusing because the word memory connotes a conscious process. The term implicit, however, indicates otherwise. While explicit memory is consciously recalled and articulated, implicit memory is experienced as an emotional reaction. We are not necessarily aware of its effect or source, yet it heavily influences our day-to-day life.

How does it do this? Deep in our emotional brain, we have three structures responsible for different types of memory, meaning-making, and emotional perception - the amygdala, the hippocampus, and the anterior cingulate. These three structures are responsible for storing and processing autobiographical memory, or memory of our personal life experience. While the hippocampus and anterior cingulate are more involved with conscious memory and meaning-making, as in recalling past life events, the amygdala's job is to store nonconscious appraisal of all our past life experiences. It uses this appraisal as programming in the neural nets of our brain to make sense of our present circumstances.

The Amygdala's Impact

---

[2] Although resources in this area are too numerous to mention, see the following for an accessible book for global understanding: Louis Cozolino, *The Neuroscience of Psychotherapy: Healing the Social Brain* (New York: W. W. Norton and Company, 2012) pg. 101.

The amygdala is only the size and shape of an almond, but its job is enormous. It stores every experience we have ever had, filed by emotional significance, as a subconscious database to help us make meaning of our current circumstances. It is constantly scanning our environment through all our senses and looking for emotional matches from experience to provide an appraisal of our present situation. For example, we perceive something as threatening, yet we are unaware of the associations our amygdala is making; we merely feel an emotional response to a present occurrence without awareness of its origination.

The amygdala's primary job is to protect us by processing vast amounts of information stored in the neural nets of our brain, looking for matches, and alerting us with an emotional response. It is not discerning and does not involve cognition. This process is beyond our awareness, which is necessary because it would be a psychological overload to be conscious of all the evaluations our amygdala is making. Its job is to protect us.

Our amygdala hijacks our emotional attention and directs it to whatever is present, similar to what has hurt us in the past. It can be as simple as a smell, gesture, sound, or behavior or as complex as a circumstance that carries familiar yet vague threatening feelings. The amygdala is not concerned with thought appraisal; its concern is mobilizing us with an emotional response to what it deems as threatening. When the amygdala evaluates a threat, the reaction is immediate. However, it is subconscious; we are unaware our present evaluation has anything to do with our emotional past.

The amygdala's job is to get our immediate attention by a "whoosh" of emotional alarm and mobilize us with fear, or fear in all its disguises (feelings of threat, anger, hate, judgments, jealousies, abandonment, etc.). And in our evolutionary past, we needed to be mobilized like this – without thought attached. For our species to survive, we needed to act, pre-thought to any perceived threat, and we only knew the danger through past programming. So, it is a fundamental protective mechanism built into our psyche; it keeps us safe by immediately repelling us from what it has been programmed to perceive as danger. The amygdala does its job well, which is vital to our survival; it is a good process. Sometimes, however, it gets out of balance and needs re-programming.

If you have consistent triggers or things that predictably activate your ingrained personal sensitivities, you likely have some of your

152

emotional programming involved. Remember, the amygdala's job isn't to rationalize; it is to act like a fire alarm to alert you that something in your present is similar to something in your past that has previously hurt you or been a threat. In addition, the more emotionally laden the previous experience is for you, the deeper it is wired into your neural nets, and the less discerning the amygdala is in its reaction. It has an inverse-response pattern: the more significant the event(s) were, the more generalized the current response is. And it is all done beyond your conscious awareness.

Further, when our amygdala is overreactive in specific areas of our life, we develop ingrained perceptions, behaviors, reactions, and sensitivities that can heavily influence or even dominate our day-to-day life. Kendra was no exception, and looking at her backstory, we can see why.

Her mother abandoned Kendra when she was young. Her father was around but primarily angry and emotionally unavailable. Her grandparents raised her, she loved them dearly, and they provided the loving connection she did not receive from her parents. However, when she was a teenager, her grandfather passed away. She had a tough time recovering from his death, and the experience resurfaced deep-seated feelings of separation and aloneness. As a result, she lived with an enduring fear of abandonment. Although she had her grandmother and many close friends who loved her deeply, her perceptions told her otherwise and blocked her receptivity to the love they offered. The challenging events in her life colored her perceptions; she did not want anyone close that could hurt or abandon her.

As she grew into an adult Kendra's amygdala network worked overtime to build walls. She did not trust anyone could love her and remain in her life. She adopted behaviors that pushed people away. Of course, this behavior only furthered her perception of abandonment, and she began to adopt beliefs like: "Everyone always leaves me" and "Nobody will ever really be there for me." She believed she would always be alone.

When her grandmother took ill, it just confirmed Kendra's deep-seated fears. Kendra was enmeshed in her perceptions of abandonment and the walls she built in defense. Where she wanted love, connection, and compassion, she could only feel fear, defensiveness, anger, and abandonment. Her implicit and neural memory clouded her perceptions to such an extent she could not be compassionate to her grandmother's plight, even when she tried to force herself.

Kendra's past and her corresponding emotional triggers severely impacted her ability to engage in her present circumstance appropriately. As a result, she needed to provide her neural programming with a new story. She needed memory reconsolidation. Before we can understand memory reconsolidation, however, it is essential to grasp the impact of our emotional triggers and how they get coded and perpetuated unless given a different opportunity.

Understanding Our Triggers

The truth is, we all evaluate our present life through the lens of our previous experiences and think we perceive reality just as it is. We all have emotional triggers that create a cascade of perceptions and reactions that may be out of context for the situation. We can often tell that it is an amygdala-driven response because the same emotional evaluation may play itself out in various circumstances of our life; words like "always" or "never" are common. Kendra felt like no one would ever be there for her.

Emotional triggers are our amygdala's way of saying "pay attention." The problem is that we don't hear it that way, and we assume the emotional lens we are looking through at that moment is the correct evaluation. Therefore, if an emotional evaluation carries a significant "felt" response or often repeats under different circumstances, it is likely an amygdala-driven response and may be out of context for the severity of the situation. Remember, our amygdala's job is to be hyperalert in evaluating threats. Still, it is often overperforming its job, and our colored perceptions become ingrained patterns of reactivity, or triggers, for us. These triggers impede our ability to be emotionally grounded and operate from our deepest self; again, they can originate from 'micro-traumas' or significant life events.

When a trigger hijacks us, we might let it consume us, try to suppress it, blame, shame, or judge ourselves for having it. None of those work, as triggers are embedded in the emotional wiring deep in the neural nets of our brain. However, memory reconsolidation can rewire them at their source. Memory reconsolidation is a process that transforms the initial coding of implicit memory in significance,

154

and subsequent impact, by providing new wiring to our neural nets. Thus, it recodes the emotional weight of the original experience and gives us emotional freedom from our triggers.

Memory Reconsolidation

For our purposes, it is helpful to look at memory reconsolidation from three vantage points: 1) How the brain initially forms to emotional experience and then re-forms with a new experience; 2) What steps research has shown are necessary to "unlock" the emotional brain, and 3) How some therapeutic techniques have approached memory reconsolidation. It all starts with our neural nets.

Neurons, Synapses, and Neural Nets

Our neural nets are clusters of neurons or nerve cells that serve as the wiring for our nervous system, including our brain. The single neurons connect through synapses, similar to little lightning bolts, that transfer information between them and create a network of stored data. This network of stored data is called a neural net and may contain 10,000 or more neurons. These neural nets wire to our experience and serve as "programming" for our brain to interpret and make sense of new events. This wiring is how we learn, and our emotional system is no different. Our neural wiring records our life experiences.

These neural nets reflect our prior experience and our ongoing thought processes, evaluations, and perceptions unless we provide for them a new experience and pattern of firing. Further, around the synapses are glial cells that function somewhat like glue. The more we have any repeated experience, and it could be just responding to an event the way we always have, the more the glial cells help facilitate long-term connections. It is often said that 'nerve cells that fire together, wire together.'

Neural nets housing implicit memory comprise our amygdala; they reflect and then record our initial experience, then file, release, and repeat according to emotional significance. So implicit memory is just neural nets wired by our past. However, if we continue to repeat our history through ingrained perceptions, predictable behavior, or reactions, our implicit memory stays programmed for reactivity.

When we routinely repeat behaviors, we further cement our neural nets' wiring, and they get more robust and more efficient at what they are programmed to do. Thus, neurally, we become better at the things we routinely do: the experiences we have, the behaviors we exhibit, the thoughts we think, and the emotions surrounding all those things. Acting, reacting, and perceiving the way we always have cultivates the capacity for more of the same. For Kendra, it was hampering her ability to live a full life and support her grandmother in the desired way. Instead of being able to respond to her grandmother in a loving and compassionate way, she reacted out of frustration and feeling imposed upon. Those reactions were the superficial responses to the deeper fears of being abandoned. And all these patterns of behavior merely reinforced her associated neural wiring.

Some approaches to healing suggest that we just 'get over' our triggers or emotional difficulties because the events that caused them are in the past, and the past is gone. However, even though the events responsible for our emotional programming are over, we are not done with them. The past may be gone, but the neural record of the event is not, and since this neural memory is wired deep within our brain, we carry it all the time. It is our constant companion, persistently filtering current circumstances yet entirely colored by the wiring of our past. Conversely, memory reconsolidation is a process of rewiring old experiences and providing new experiences in the depths of our neural networks. We are 'un-learning' one perceptual framework and re-learning another. This rewiring is where the hope lies.

The Role of Neuroplasticity

Although it is often said that 'nerve cells that fire together, wire together,' it is also true that 'nerve cells that no longer fire together no longer wire together. Our science used to tell us that once nerve cells wire for connection, they maintain that connection. Now we know that assumption was false due to the discovery of neuroplasticity. Neuroplasticity means that neural connections are not hard-wired or permanent. Instead, when established neural links cease to fire through repeated experience, the old neural relationship breaks its bond in the neural net, and another bond forms. In other words, the brain can reorganize synaptic connections, and thus entire neural nets, with a new experience.

It is important to note, however, that suppressing a response does not break the original neural relationship. Neural connections, especially those associated with emotional events, are formed deep in our brain in response to our authentic experience of those events. Supression comes from a different part of the brain, and therefore doesn't reform the associated neural nets. In other words, the problematic emotional or implicit memory needs to be transformed at its source, or where the traumatic memory is wired. In Kendra's case pretending her past didn't exist wouldn't work. She needed to access the implicit memory where it was stored and give her neural nets a different experience. That process is called memory reconsolidation.

Memory reconsolidation is neuroplasticity in the context of emotional or implicit memory. While neuroplasticity can refer to the whole nervous system, memory reconsolidation is the reorganization of emotional memory. It is a process by which the initial coding of implicit memory transforms in significance, and subsequent impact, by providing new wiring to our emotional neural nets. We are replacing the 'wiring' of past experiences, even deep traumatic ones, with new and functional wiring. Thus, it recodes the emotional weight of the original experience and provides us emotional freedom from our triggers. Our brain is a verb. Memory reconsolidation allows us to replace old and harmful emotional programming with new and healthy neural wiring. And imagery can be the conduit. In Kendra's case she began to use deep imagery to reconsolidate her problematic implicit memory, and used the specific steps outlined below.

Unlocking the Implicit

In memory reconsolidation, specific steps help to rescript the troublesome neural wiring[3]. First, at some level, we need to engage the old neural wiring without letting it consume us. This engagement helps us access or 'unlock' it. Further, it does not need

---

[3] Bruce Ecker, "Memory reconsolidation understood and misunderstood". *International Journal of Neuropsychotherapy* 3,1.(2015): p. 2-46.

to be a conscious recollection of the actual memory. In other words, accessing a connected feeling or image may be enough to stimulate the correlated neural nets without remembering a specific event. For example, Kendra didn't necessarily need to recount all the specifics of her story (although she could have if she wanted to); she just needed to access the associated emotions without letting them consume her. She could have shared her feelings, a symbolic image, or a representative story. The critical concept is stimulating the associated neural nets just enough to 'open' them for rewiring. This 'unlocks' it, if you will, and allows us to rewire a new experience[4].

Second, we need to change our typical response. Remember, responding in the ways we always have just solidifies our wired response patterns. Merely stopping our habitual response changes the coding of our neural nets and primes them for a different experience. Further, holding ourselves in a self-compassionate understanding creates a neural state more conducive to change; rewiring works more efficiently when we are nonreactive. Also, it can be helpful to appreciate that implicit memory is a process designed to keep us safe, even if it is out of balance now. We can understand how and why it was stored in the first place and provide ourselves the compassion we would for a best friend with the same difficulties.

Third, we need to offer a mismatch of implicit memory. In other words, we give our neural nets a different response by imagining an alternative experience. For example, we envision an experience that meets our underlying healing needs. In Kendra's case she imagined her adult self giving her young self the love she needed and wanted from her mother, but never received. We can, most of the time, identify that underlying need through an associated image, feeling, or intuitive knowing. In essence, we hold ourselves in a self-compassionate awareness and listen to what the vision, memory, or feeling is trying to convey about what it needs now, or needed then, for healing to occur. As you will see shortly, the Compassion Practice incorporates all these steps.

Remember, trauma is no longer in the previous event but our neural nets. Our neural networks store all the micro to major traumas of our life, and, with new experiences, we can re-program

[4] Bruce Ecker, R Ticic, L Hulley, *Unlocking the Emotional Brain: Eliminating Symptoms at their Roots Using Memory Consolidation* (New York: Routledge, 2012).

them. Because the brain does not know the difference between what we vividly imagine and what is real, through imagery, we can rescript the emotional "hold" of our past and create an improved meaning-making center in our brain. We retain the conscious or explicit memory of the event but are no longer consumed by its charge.

Memory Rescripting and the Healing of Memories

Various therapies and contemplative practices have used memory reconsolidation as a mechanism of healing for over a century and under many different name[5]. Memory rescripting, image rescripting, or the healing of memories are a few terms ascribed to these practices. However, although they have appeared under various names and associated techniques, the underlying process is very similar.

When used therapeutically, this underlying process typically involves inviting the client to access a problematic emotion or traumatic memory through deep imagery and providing a different outcome. First, the client engages the memory just enough to slightly re-experience it, but not so much that they are flooded or retraumatized. Then, after the client accesses the memory "enough," they "rescript" the memory in a comfortable and healing way.

---

[5] The dynamics of healing in the Compassion practice is based heavily on memory re-scripting. See the following references for the many ways imagery has been used in therapeutic healing: David Edwards, "Restructuring implicational meaning through memory-based imagery: Some historical notes". *Journal on Behavior Therapy and Experimental Psychiatry* 38, 4 (2008): p. 306-16; Arnoud Arntz, "Imagery Rescripting as a Therapeutic Technique: Review of Clinical Trials, Basic Studies, and Research Agenda" *Journal of Experimental Psychopathology* 3, 2 (2012): p. 189-208; E. A. Holmes, A Arntz, M. R. Smucker, "Imagery rescripting in cognitive behaviour the images, treatment techniques and outcomes" *Journal of Behavior Therapy an Experimental Psychiatry* 38, 4 (2007): p. 297-305; S Rahnama, M. Tarkhan, J. Khalatbari "Effectivenes of imagery rescripting and reprocesing therapy on suicidal ideation in individuals with suicide attempt history" *Procedia - Social and Behavioral Sciences* 84, 9 (2012): p. 1095-1099; C. Slofstra, M. H. Nauta, E. A. Holmes, C. L. Bockting " Imagery rescripting: The impact of conceptual and perceptual changes on avrsive autobiographical memories" *PloS One* 11, 8 (2016); M. R. Smucker, C. V. Dancu, E. B. Foa, J. Niederee "Imagery re-scripting: a new treatment for survivors of childhood sexual abuse suffering from post traumatic stress" *Journal of Cognitive Psychotherapy: An International Quarterly* 9, 1 (1995): p. 3-17; J. Wild, D. M. Clark, "Imagery rescripting of early traumatic memories in social phobia" *Cognitive Behavioral Practice* 18, 4 (2011): p. 433-443.

For instance, this imagery may involve visions of them as a child in a distressing event and then as an adult coming into the scene and changing the outcome. Although this is just an example, these techniques have been used in various circumstances and often solicited impressive results. One of my favorite examples is the story of a man who was a child in the Holocaust. When horrific images resurfaced for him as an adult, he would deeply imagine a magical tricycle swooping down and taking him away from the terror. Through this process, he relaxed the traumatic, embodied reaction of the memory but kept the autobiographical narrative surrounding it, and his PTSD began to subside[6]. In other words, he could recall the events without being emotionally hijacked by his response.

Additionally, there is evidence that the rescripted memory doesn't have to be based on conscious recollection[7]. A representative image of the memory will suffice if it stimulates the associated neural networks. We may not have access to the conscious memory for various reasons, including suppression, it being preverbal, an inability to identify a source of our difficult feeling, etc. Also, it may not be wise to use the conscious memory if it is too traumatizing. That is not necessary. A symbolic image will work if it is representative of our emotional experience.

How, then, do we heal? First, we heal by going to the source. We heal by creating new and healing experiences; these new experiences restore clear vision to a clouded and triggered system and rewire our problematic neural nets at their origin. Second, appropriately applied self-compassion practices can provide that experience through contemplative practice. Simply put, we can rewire our neural networks through meditation and imagination to take the emotional charge out of those triggers that discolor and disrupt our lives. Memory reconsolidation provides the scientific explanation of the healing potential of techniques such as the Compassion Practice.

The Basic Foundations of the Compassion Practice

6 Louis Cozolino, *The Neuroscience of Psychotherapy: Healing the Social Brain* (New York: W. W. Norton and Company, 2012) pg. 101.
7 C. Slofstra, M. H. Nauta, E. A. Holmes, C. L. Bockting "Imagery rescripting: The impact of conceptual and perceptual changes on avrsive autobiographical memories" *PloS One* 11, 8 (2016).

Following, I present the essential characteristics of the Compassion Practice. First is how I believe Frank would describe them, and second is my rewording/re-capping in the context of this chapter.

Frank: We all have a best self. When we are grounded in our best selves, we flourish and function at our highest emotional potential. This best self is our natural state, and when we are not in it, we are activated by an internal movement that is yearning for healing.

Alane: Internal movements are wired perceptions and interpretations deep in our brain's neural nets. They present as emotional triggers caused by problematic experiences and implicit memory. They will continue to knock us off our best selves until our neural nets rewire through a new and healing experience.

Frank: When an internal movement activates us, the invitation is to take a U-turn or look back within ourselves, and with non-judgmental, mindful awareness, recognize that it is rooted in a deep desire for healing and should be welcomed with understanding.

Alane: These internal movements form from the challenging experiences of our lives or the behaviors, reactions, or choices we have adopted to protect them; when they are out of balance, we need to rewire them. Further, although out of balance now and likely not appropriate for the current situation, we can appreciate that the original process was to protect us, and approach these internal movements with love and understanding.

Frank: We can tend these interior movements with self-compassion. From the intuitive knowings of our best self and a sacred resource, if appropriate, we can be guided by self-compassionate imagery to heal and rebalance the wounds of our past.

Alane: Self-compassionate imagery rewires the neural memory of our painful past through memory reconsolidation. Thus, our emotional systems rebalance, and we are provided emotional freedom from our triggers.

Frank Rogers came upon the foundations of the Compassion Practice through inner work and deep healing surrounding childhood adversity. His friends and colleagues helped him define the process and give it a name. Even though his journey was organic in nature and full of trial and error, he found a path to healing. That path to healing holds up to a scientific understanding of emotional regeneration.

The Compassion Practice invites us into a process of self-compassion and, from there, invites us to expand those sensibilities to others. Although Kendra did not do the Compassion Practice, per se, her process was similar.

Kendra had various internal movements controlling her present. She was profoundly scared and sincerely felt no one would ever be there for her. She was self-protective and wary of being abandoned again; she often 'left' anyone that did get close before they could leave her. She built walls and went numb. These walls prevented her from being with her grandmother in any compassionate way, and she hated herself for them.

Kendra knew she needed to heal before losing her grandmother and any capability to spend her last precious months with her. So, she began to use intentional practice and imagery to help her heal. Her practice for healing went something like this:

She began the process by settling into her breath and noticing the activity of her thoughts, emotions, and bodily sensations from a witnessing, non-judgmental and observing point of view. She approached her internal process with self-understanding and compassion. Feeling secure and protected, she allowed herself to feel the 'nudging' of the familiar sense of abandonment from a grounded space without letting it overwhelm her. By engaging this internal movement 'just enough,' she could 'unlock' the emotional memories surrounding it without allowing them to flood her. This 'unlocking' gave her the answer.

She imagined she had a "twin" that she loved dearly, and that twin needed to tell her story. Deep in meditation, Kendra could fully maintain a witnessing perspective and entirely hear and hold her personal story as told by her fictitious twin. She attended and witnessed the traumatic events of her life while maintaining emotional stability and a sense of separate groundedness. Once she wholly saw her fictional twin's story, still deep in meditative space, she asked her "twin" what she needed for healing. Using deep imagery, complete with a felt sense of love, compassion, and connection, she imagined the core of her best self, providing her young "twin" the love, relationship, and healing she desperately needed and should have gotten as a child. She was all at once the giver and the receiver, and she could genuinely experience a sense of deep healing. She gave herself the love and security she should have gotten as a child. And her neural networks wired to the new experience.

For Kendra, the healing experience was palpable, and she felt an emotional weight lifted to such an extent she could be fully there for her grandmother. Further, through the understanding of her own experience, she could find compassion for her grandmother's past as well. The mother that had abandoned Kendra was the daughter that had abandoned her grandmother. The grandfather that died and left her full of grief was the husband of her grieving grandmother. Kendra was able to see her grandmother and her grandmother's difficulties in a whole new light.

Bibliography

Arntz, Arnoud. "Imagery Rescripting as a Therapeutic Technique: Review of Clinical Trials, Basic Studies, and Research Agenda." *Journal of Experimental Psychopathology* 3, 2 (2012): 189-208.

Cozolino, Louis. *The Neuroscience of Psychotherapy: Healing the Social Brain*. New York: W. W. Norton and Company, 2012.

Ecker, Bruce, R Ticic, and L Hulley. *Unlocking the Emotional Brain: Eliminating Symptoms at their Roots Using Memory Consolidation*. New York: Routledge, 2012.

Ecker, Bruce. "Memory reconsolidation understood and misunderstood." *International Journal of Neuropsychotherapy* 3,1 (2015): 2-46.

Edwards, David. "Restructuring implicational meaning through memory-based imagery: Some historical notes." *Journal on Behavior Therapy and Experimental Psychiatry* 38, 4 (2008): 306-16.

Holmes, E. A., A Arntz, and M. R. Smucker. "Imagery rescripting in cognitive behaviour the images, treatment techniques and outcomes." *Journal of Behavior Therapy an Experimental Psychiatry* 38, 4 (2007): 297-305.

Rahnama, S, M. Tarkhan, and J. Khalatbari. "Effectiveness of imagery rescripting and reprocessing therapy on suicidal ideation in individuals with suicide attempt history." *Procedia - Social and Behavioral Sciences* 84, 9 (2012): 1095-1099;

Rogers, Frank. *Compassion in Practice: The Way of Jesus*. Nashville, TN: Upper Room Books, 2016.

Rogers, Frank. *Practicing Compassion*. Nashville, TN: Fresh Air Books, 2015.

Slofstra, C., M. H. Nauta, E. A. Holmes, and C. L. Bockting. "Imagery rescripting: The impact of conceptual and perceptual changes on aversive autobiographical memories." *PloS One* 11, 8 (2016).

Smucker, M. R., C. V. Dancu, E. B. Foa, and J. Niederee. "Imagery re-scripting: a new treatment for survivors of childhood sexual abuse suffering from post traumatic stress." *Journal of Cognitive Psychotherapy: An International Quarterly* 9, 1 (1995): 3-17.

Wild, J., and D. M. Clark. "Imagery rescripting of early traumatic memories in social phobia." *Cognitive Behavioral Practice* 18, 4 (2011): 433-443.

Where the Flowers Grow: A Personal Tribute

Andy Dreitcer

Author's note: The versions of the stories I'm about to tell are full of facts — as I remember them. I hope Frank's memories match mine. In any case, I am sure that Frank's versions of the stories would be the True ones.

Frank and I were on our way home from a multi-day meeting in Indianapolis. That event – almost thirty years ago now -- had drawn together the directors of a number of Lilly-Endowment-funded projects. The purpose of the meeting: "networking and mutual edification," Not really my cup of tea. My kind of introvert doesn't really go in for a lot of networking, let alone mutual edification, at least in the buttoned-up, dispassionate, circle-of-academics version I expected to unfold in that hotel conference room over those three days. But as it turned out, edifying networking actually did happen for me – though it didn't unfold as I had feared. Instead of entering into processes of strut-your-stuff academics, I met Frank. And looking back, I can see that was the beginning of the end for me, the end of a problematic way of perceiving and thinking and feeling that I had not even realized held me in its grip. Meeting Frank positively changed my life, and would continue to change my life for decades to come. But I'm getting ahead of myself. For now, let me stick to the facts of this story I'm trying to tell. So, yes, I met Frank. And honest-to-God networking and edification ensued. Which meant that I was very happy to learn that on the first leg of our individual journeys home we would be traveling together.

On our flight out of Indy, traveling together, before transferring to the separate, second legs of our trips (Frank's to Los Angeles; mine to San Francisco), we managed to get seats next to each other, which gave us time for a long chat. Our few days of sharing time in the Heartland[1] had shown me how our interests, sensibilities, and vocations aligned. Yes, we were both receiving Lilly funding for

---

[1] Frank, as you may know, is a big fan of hearts. And yes, "sharing time in the Heartland" aptly names what my years of friendship and colleagueship with Frank feel like.

youth-ministry-related spirituality projects in a seminary, but I learned we had so much more in common than that: a passion for following the soul's quest to engage Sacred Mystery; a trust that personal healing can come through spiritual companionship; a commitment to the social-cultural transformation that can flow from contemplation-grounded activism; engagement with spiritual practices that make new life possible; a fan-boy attachment to monasticism; explorations of the powerful truths (and the destructive twisting of those truths) that can be found in every profound spiritual tradition. We talked non-stop, focused on what was vital to us. And somewhere toward the end of our flight, Frank turned to me and said, "We are going to work together someday."

That "someday" came about seven years later. A new position opened up at Claremont School of Theology: Director of Spiritual Formation and professor in the field of Spirituality. Frank was on the search committee -- and soon on the phone with me. Then I was in Claremont for a daylong interview. And...I bombed. Truly. Totally bombed. I can still find the crater marks on the campus. Frank's compassionate (and continuing) take on the interview: "Dude. You stunk." Can you believe he said that? Okay, you're right. Frank did not, would never, say something like that. It just felt like that at the time, because even Frank couldn't shape my crash-and-burn into a hopeful story. What he actually said (and does to this day) in that gentle, Frank way of his, was this: "Well, it seemed like you weren't really at your best." Dagger to the heart. *Et tu,* Frank? "Were you okay? I was kind of worried about you. What happened?" What happened? Well, you know, the usual: I hadn't had enough water, wrong color of shirt, not enough protein, I was cold, the sun was too bright, there were people, I was hot, it was a Tuesday, my shoes were too tight, there were florescent lights, I didn't have my lucky charm, I should get a lucky charm, I saw mountains in the distance, my socks were too loose, did I mention it was a Tuesday, or maybe a Thursday, or possibly a day that ends in 'y'? You see the problem: I had bombed. But in the end, I had two things going for me: (1) The faculty had decided that *all* of the candidates had bombed, (2) Frank still believed in me, and convinced the search committee to give me, and only me, another interview.

As it turned out, this would be the second time (with more to come) that Frank changed my life. The first: on that flight home from

Indianapolis, he had offered me confirmation that my life's commitments were true and good and life-giving, even in the midst of a time of doubts and regrets and more pain than I felt I could carry. And now he would make a way for me where there was no way. He would clear a new vocational path, life path, for me. At Frank's urging, and trusting Frank's instincts (as many rightly have before and after), the search committee flew me to a secret interview at a location near the airport, ten miles from Claremont. And in that ninety-minute meeting at the turn of the millennium, Frank led us all in a process of uncovering the ways I could meet the academic and programmatic needs laid out in the position description. And lo, a miracle came to pass. Thank Frank, the job was mine. In spite of my worst efforts, Frank had taken me from cratering to colleague.

Truth be told, I can go a bit bonkers if I sink very far into the thought of what might have been. Had Frank not believed in me through those interviews, for the past 23 years I would have lived a sadly different life. Frank saved me from that, probably saving my sanity and more in the process. He saw the best in me. Coaxed that into the open. Helped it flourish. Of course, I am not unique in that. To know Frank is to know that this is Frank's way with people, with students, faculty colleagues, friends, spiritual directees, the broken, the lost, the soul-sick, the haters, the seekers, the psychologically wounded, the sad, the happy, those he's only read about and will never meet, those far away, and those very close at hand.[2] Frank, and only Frank, will bring chocolate to the staff as a holiday gift. Frank will sit with you in the hard times and lead you to play when the time is right (more on that later). Frank will ask you how you are in passing, and really mean it. And you will stop and tell him. And he will listen with a smile that is shaped the way everyone else in the world frowns, with the corners of the mouth downturned. (Somehow, Frank manages to transform even the traditional frown-shape into a comforting, compassionate *smile.*) And then you will feel better. For you will have tasted some truth about yourself, the world, life and love, and what it means to experience compassion not only for others, but for yourself and all creation. You have glimpsed the part of you that Frank sees: that sacred core of

---

[2] But not the Los Angeles Dodgers. Frank and I laugh about the fact that the Dodgers serve as his foil, a safe place into which he can dump any of the animosities that linger in the Shadows of his soul.

creativity and compassion, that deep longing for the good and true, that urge to be free and to help others find freedom, as well.

But again, I digress. Let's get back to the story.

"We are going to work together someday." Now, finally, that "someday" had come. This was my chance to start anew after many discouraging, debilitating years in another institution. The two of us, Frank and I, would create amazing spiritual things together -- unique programs, unparalleled learning environments, formational opportunities that would draw people from far and wide. At the first faculty meeting I attended, the pre-semester retreat, I was welcomed with open arms as the new guy on the block. I expressed my thanks and my eagerness to do whatever I could for the benefit of the CST community. When Frank's turn to speak came, I waited for the profound words that would propel the two of us forward and upward to previously-unrealized spiritual heights. Finally, Frank spoke: "I want you all to know that I have come to a very difficult decision. I've spent months in discernment about this. And here it is: I'm resigning my position at CST, effective immediately."

What??!! Bait and switch! Stunned, heart-broken, baffled, I struggled to understand why my friend, my new colleague, would do this to me, abandon me. Shocker: it wasn't about me. Instead, it was about Frank following his soul's desire, his heart's longing. Frank wanted, needed, two years to write the novel that had been taking shape in him. And from what I understood, he simply could not do that and fulfill his job responsibilities. In addition, he had come to feel that academia simply did not have a place for what was most vocationally dear to him – individual and social transformation through the contemplative power of stories. Hard as it was to grasp, here was Frank's third gift to me: A demonstration of what it means to step out in faith, responding to a Divine tug, clear-eyed and courageous, with no firm notion of where money, support, even meals would come from in the years ahead. Frank was, is, that committed to what gives every person, every soul, life.

It turned out that the faculty members and the administration simply wouldn't let Frank go. With strong encouragement from the faculty, the Dean found grant money and a donor to allow Frank to do part-time special projects at CST while he focused on his novel. And after two or three years of writing, he returned full time to the faculty, with a new portfolio, one that more fully matched the vital skills and sensibilities Frank brings to academia, and that academia desperately needs. When Frank came back, the fun began – at least for me.

Upon Frank's return, we began to dream, to plan, to create. Something had been brewing in Frank for years. It had to do with a thing he called "The Three-Fold Spiritual Path," with Contemplation, Creativity, and Compassion inseparably intertwined to create individual, relational, structural, cultural, and social healing, freedom, and transformation. For Frank this defined the true heart of Christian spirituality and connected the truths in that tradition with the truths in others. I was all in. But before we could begin planning in earnest, my energies were diverted to family matters when my spouse became seriously ill. Frank, of course, became a rock for me in that time, even covering my course when my wife passed away in the middle of a semester. So, it wasn't until 2005 that we were able to fully begin our planning together.

To workshop the Three-Fold Path, we developed and co-taught a series of courses, including "Spiritual Formation for the Contemplative Way" (focusing on contemplative practice traditions), "Spiritual Formation for Personal and Relational Vitality" (primarily engaging processes of creativity), and "Spiritual Formation for Compassionate Social Engagement" (highlighting compassionate transformations of relationships and systems). We also created a thing we called Triptykos, as we joined forces with a good friend and colleague, Mark Yaconelli.[3] For us, Triptykos was our living expression of a three-panel icon that held not only the three of us, but the Three-Fold Spiritual Path we were committed to refining and teaching.

Triptykos brought many adventures, including: crashing on hotel room cots during a shoestring-budget trip seeking funding for our work (we got it!); presenting compassion practices to congressional representatives in D.C. (not so sure they got it!); developing a compassion curriculum for prison ministries throughout Canada; compassion-related conferences, meetings, and trips in Northern Ireland, Zimbabwe, Israel, England, Iceland, and throughout the United States. Out of the work of Triptykos and the

---

[3] Mark and I ran a youth-ministry-related, Lilly-Endowment-funded spirituality project at another seminary. After I met Frank, he accepted an invitation from Mark and me to be on the advisory board for that project.

courses we taught, came the Compassion Practice and the Center for Engaged Compassion.

But creating the Compassion Practice itself took much time and energy. And in the end, it sneaked up on us, as it had never been part of our original plan. As I've noted, we were teaching courses to refine our understanding and presentations of the Three-Fold Spiritual Path. That involved engaging class participants in innumerable spiritual practices from contemplative traditions. I began to notice a trend: no matter what practice tradition we taught, whether apophatic or kataphatic, Frank always moved it to a kataphatic conclusion. For example, within Christian Centering Prayer or in various Buddhist-based mindfulness practices, the process of releasing images and feelings inevitably led Frank to deep explorations of those very images and feelings — which seemed to me to be the opposite of what those traditions prescribed. This (seeming) disjunction came to a head during one class time when we were describing to the students the tradition of labyrinth meditation. Someone asked, "When you get to the center of the labyrinth, what do you do with the images and feelings that have come to you?" Our simultaneous responses: "Let it go!" (Andy); "Pray that!" (Frank). We looked at each other and laughed. That was the breakthrough we needed.

Back in Frank's office after class I started probing the source of his "incorrect" interpretation of the traditions. That included asking him about the thing he was always referring to in passing as "my practice." It turned out that Frank began each day with a practice he had developed over time as a way of healing trauma and giving him life. Across many years of deep exploration of many, many practice traditions, he had gathered into one practice what he found to be the most powerfully transformative dimensions of those traditions. After pushing him to describe that practice in detail, and suspecting it was the foundation not only for his teaching and his professional passion, but for his way of life, I suggested that this practice was what we needed to focus on. Frank, ever humble, wasn't so sure. It was just his little idiosyncratic thing; why would anyone else be interested in or helped by it?

It so happened that we had scheduled a three-day planning retreat for a weekend soon after this breakthrough. Frank, Mark, and I gathered with three other friends to develop a way forward for the Three-Fold Path. During the last few hours of the retreat,

Frank and I rather hesitantly introduced our thoughts about his practice, suggesting to the group that we might be able to create from it a teachable core process for our work. Then Frank's atomized description of the practice (nudged along by our unrelenting 'then what happens?') inspired new focus and renewed energy. In a matter of a few hours we tore that practice to bits — and then started to reconstruct it as something that someone less embedded in it than Frank could enter into with minimal guidance. With relentless whittling, winnowing, and reworking, we got the thing down to 26 main moves, with scores of sub-moves under each of the 26. For Frank, of course, his practice simply flowed. But the more we worked with it the more we recognized how subtle, multidimensional, and complex it was. And the more impossible the teaching of it seemed. How could we capture, let alone teach, such a thing as this?

But in the weeks and months after that retreat, the effort to formulate a teachable Compassion Practice (the temporary name we gave the thing at the end of our three days together) consumed much of our —and especially Frank's — creative energy. Frank filled paper notebooks with arrows and circles and illegible (to mortal eyes) words in a search to identify and accurately name each step. I created electronic charts and spreadsheets listing the many tradition-streams that the practice encapsulated and the neurophysiological capacities it drew upon and honed. Mark road-tested dozens of terms and concepts at retreats and seminars, watching for the ones that clicked. At one point we had named over a dozen primary steps to the practice with terms that proceeded in alphabetical order. That led to a dead end, along with many other paths. Finally, though, a eureka moment. I paced the back deck of our home, phone to my ear in a conference call, as Frank told Mark and me that he had found the acronym that precisely captured a key movement of the practice.[4] From that point the creative process unfolded more steadily and clearly, as the Compassion Practice came more fully (albeit slowly) into being. And over time Triptykos was replaced by The Center for Engaged Compassion, with the

---

[4] F.L.A.G. signals this process, in brief: After you have identified a particular interior movement (feeling, thought, sensation, etc.) that has you in its grasp, imagine that movement as a being, creature, or other entity, and have a conversation with it – and ask what it Fears, what Longing it experiences, what deep Ache it holds, and/or what stifled or unrealized Gift it carries.

Three-Fold Path integrated into the processes of compassion formation through the Compassion Practice.

All along we were very clear that the description we finally formulated was not the entirety of the practice itself. Rather, it was and is but one attempt to convey, to teach, to pass on, a healing, empowering, freeing experience of the Mysterious Presence of Divine Compassion. The words we came to for The Compassion Practice attempted to convey the ineffable. So they will never be enough. Still, certain core characteristics remain, dimensions of experience or ways of being that flow from deeply engaging in the Practice and that are uniquely shaped by the contexts in which they live. Two of these characteristics — shaped within quite divergent contexts — particular stand out as important for my own life.

The first of these core characteristics has to do with the ways creativity can unleash personal freedom for the joyful expression of gifts that have been unrecognized or squelched. One dimension of practice connected to this is playfulness. If you have seen Frank with teenagers (or at baseball games), you know of his passion for play. Over the years he has concocted elaborate games and adventures for the teens in his life, not only for his son and friends in times past, but for the participants in the youth ministry programs he has designed or led, and the community center after-school theater program he developed for underprivileged teenagers. Faculty colleagues who departed our seminary have been blessed at going-away parties with detailed skits reflecting their life and work. Frank has been known to write music, sing, take on the persona of celebrities (a Bruce Springsteen imitation comes to mind), and generally invite everyone present to join the fun.

Frank brought this playfulness to the course we taught on spiritual formation and creative vitality. We assigned (or rather, Frank came up with, and I enthusiastically embraced) a capstone project for the course: each student was to engage in a creative process throughout the semester, leading to a class exhibition of all projects in the chapel on the final day of the course. One student learned to quilt. Another made a movie. Still another took oil-painting lessons. Everyone in the course fully engaged the assignment, bringing quilts, movies, paintings, whatever they had created out of the vitality of their lives.

Frank and I decided that it was only fair that we create and exhibit a project as well. So we chose to perform a song and dance

172

routine as the "Muse Brothers." (DVD's exist that carry recordings of this. Bonus points to anyone who can find one.) Frank re-wrote the lyrics to popular songs, filling them with a compassion theme. And he helped me learn (sort of) to play the harmonica. He already knew how, of course. So he was the main musician. I was the choreographer. Neighbors who happened to glance through Frank's living room picture window as they passed his house in the evening were amazed to see us practicing line dances. And I have to say, when exhibition day came, we smashed it. Frank entered with a cartwheel and took the lead on harp and vocals. I danced behind him and up and down the chapel aisle -- when we weren't line-dancing or playing harmonica duets. Students gaped, stunned, then joined the fun. Rave reviews followed. Frank's gift to me that semester: dropping pretensions and fears, letting creativity and fun flow, embracing freedom and untapped skills, learning what it felt like to cut loose and play in a way that feeds us, body and soul.

The second core characteristic that I especially value also involves freedom — the profound liberation of communities and systems, as well as individuals. We were invited by one of our former PhD students, Mazvita Machinga, to help her lead a conference on healing and reconciliation through the pastoral counseling center she had founded in Zimbabwe. The government at the time had established a Ministry of Healing and Reconciliation, and invited organizations to develop programming and processes aligned with that theme. Everyone in the country feared the invitation was nothing but a way for Robert Mugabe's sanctioned thugs to identify and clamp down on suspected dissidents. So no one in the country responded to the invitation — except Mazvita Machinga. So Frank, Mark, and I soon found ourselves in Matare with Dr. Machinga. Also with her: over ninety tribal leaders, Christian pastors, and church laypersons, along with two government spies. (Government officials had been invited, but somehow those in power felt it more appropriate to send undercover agents instead of official representatives.) As far as anyone knew, this was the first time Zimbabwean tribal and Christian leaders had ever come together to collaborate for the common good. And it was certainly the first gathering in Zimbabwe meant to address healing and reconciliation. The participants had traveled for days, struggling to find the funds to attend, hoping to learn how they could faithfully respond to Divine calls to forgive — even under the most horrific of circumstances.

How horrific were their circumstances? The participants in the conference had seen family members and friends tortured, raped, and killed during the last national election, as President Mugabe worked to "persuade" citizens to vote for him. In fact, many of those present had themselves been tortured, with some left for dead. To add to the horror, the perpetrators of the violence were young men who had grown up in the villages they terrorized. In the midst of 95% unemployment, Mugabe's government had coerced these young men with money and alcohol to do its dirty work. Now that the election was over, these despised individuals, many of them only teenagers, had nowhere to go but the villages they grew up in – among the very people they had recently terrorized. The conference participants – spiritual leaders who preached forgiveness – longed to learn how they could actually forgive the perpetrators of these atrocities.

In the face of this challenge, Frank and Mazvita remained undaunted. Drawing on the dynamics of the Compassion Practice, and guided by Mazvita's understanding of the situations of the conference participants, the two of them led the group through a three-day process that ended with the leaders from each village designing a community-wide, multi-year restorative justice program tailored to the unique needs of the various contexts. At the same time, Frank was meeting with a group of torture survivors. A number were missing index fingers that had been removed when these brave souls had refused to say they would vote for Mugabe; those mutilations meant these faithful citizens were not able to offer the fingerprints required to record official votes against Mugabe. Frank led this group in processes for compassionately exploring and beginning to heal the trauma they endured.

The personal and communal work carried out in these few days powerfully demonstrated the liberating power of Frank's practice, presence, and very life. What he models and teaches offers openings for the transformative healing of horror-shaped traumas – not only for individuals, but for the systems and communities within which individuals search for life in the face of death.

As the situations described above suggest, the brilliance Frank brings to the world includes his ability to incorporate a plethora of seemingly disparate elements, human capacities, and formative

174

experiences similarly powerful movements toward compassion. Whether filling a seminary classroom with song and dance or offering tortured individuals and communities a path to healing freedom, Frank always shows up as the creative, contemplative, compassionate companion on the Way.

Frank's ability to incorporate seemingly dissimilar elements of human experience appears within his own life of spiritual practice. I have come to see that in his personal daily practice — a version of the thing the rest of us know as The Compassion Practice — Frank has, through years of trial and error, meticulously and intentionally drawn together the most powerfully formative elements found in the global history of practice traditions. So it is no accident that in The Compassion Practice we find a seamless integration of the core human capacities that most effectively shape compassion[5]:

1. *Conceptual Framings* and explicitly stated *Assumptions* guide intentions, expectations, and aspirations: In teaching The Compassion Practice, Frank tells stories, describes underlying perspectives, provides information and insights, and guides understandings of how and why the process unfolds.

2. *Grounding* or centering allows for fully settling into the present time and place: The most common entry into The Compassion Practice takes the form of Frank's invitation to "catch your breath"; deep, gentle breathing is an extraordinarily effect route to neurophysiological relaxation and mental quietude.

3. *Awareness* and *Attention* surface, identify, and name the deepest movements within human experience, mapping territory to be explored: In the Practice, Frank invites us to notice what feeling, thought, or sensation is most alive in the moment, and to focus our attention on that movement so that we can begin to (be)hold it with compassion.

---

[5] I am skimming over the details of The Compassion Practice in this section and in the one that follows, as my intention is not to describe, deconstruct, or interpret the Practice *per se* but to point to what it reveals about Frank's own skills and sensibilities in creating and teaching it. For detailed expositions of the Practice see Frank Rogers, Jr., *The Way of Jesus: Compassion in Practice* (Nashville: Upper Room Books, 2016) and *Practicing Compassion* (Nashville: Fresh Air Books, 2015). For an exploration of the Christian roots of the Practice and its commonalities with practices from other spiritual traditions see Andrew Dreitcer, *Living Compassion: Loving Like Jesus.* (Nashville: Upper Room Books, 2017).

4. *Imagination, Emotions,* and felt *Intimacy* do the direct work of constructing compassion: Frank encourages compassion-seekers to imagine and feel their way into a new way of being, a renewed intimacy with the Sacred, themselves, others, and the world. For Frank, these images, affections, and experiences of deep relationship carry the power that creates the felt sense of compassion within the moments of The Compassion Practice itself. In so doing, they build the muscles that allow us to activate compassion in our daily lives in the world.

5. Information-fed, wisdom-filled *Discernment* points the way toward lived possibilities: In the Practice, Frank follows spiritual traditions that insist true compassion will not come to pass unless wise discernment lays out an intentional path forward.

6. Concrete *Behaviors* embody compassion: For Frank, true compassion does not exist unless it comes alive in the world. Compassion is not only an aspiration, a hope, an idea, an image, or a feeling. It must be enacted in a behavior – even if that behavior is thoughtfully, intentional embodiment restraint, something that looks like no action. For this reason, The Compassion Practice ends not in aspiration or intention (as other compassion-cultivating practices do), but in some kind of intentional engagement directed toward the possibility of personal, relational, or structural change.

In addition to filling The Compassion Practice with the core compassion-forming human capacities outlined above (and common to a multitude of spiritual traditions) Frank has infused it with spiritual practice skills and sensibilities of a number of Christian practice traditions. In order to offer a taste of the depth and breadth of Frank's spiritual quest and understanding, I'll name-drop a number of traditions that serve as fonts for Frank's life and work, especially as that shows up in The Compassion Practice:

- Drawing on the early Desert tradition of *Prayer of the Heart*, Medieval practices of *Recollection*, and contemporary *Centering Prayer*, The Compassion Practice *grounds* us in the Presence of Compassion.
- The Compassion Practice turns us to a Divinely-grounded *self-compassion*, as it draws on the ancient invitation of the *Jesus Prayer* to "place the mind in the heart."

- Reflecting the process of the Medieval Franciscan *Meditations on the Life of Christ* and the sixteenth-century *Spiritual Exercises of St. Ignatius*, the Practice uses imagination and affections to create in us intimate feelings of *compassion for others* — even when we experience those others as enemies.
- Sharing the sensibilities of "The Contemplation to Attain Love" described in the *Ignatian Exercises*, the Practice invites us to an abiding stance of engaged, active, embodied *compassion toward things in the universe.*

In spite of the richness all I've outlined above, compassion formation is, let's face it, all but impossible — or so I had always believed. Then Frank turned that around for me. Frank's teaching offers almost endless invitations, limitless entry points for becoming a compassionate soul. Two of these portals to compassion drew me in. If you know the Practice, maybe you, too, have found them life-changing.

The first is The Compassion Practice's version of "less is more." The Practice asks me to imagine and attend to nothing but a single piece of experience at a time — one feeling, one thought, one sensation — rather than focus on the entire person as one big chunk. I found it was much easier to bring compassion to a part of myself or another person than to the whole complex, often-unlikable tangle of a stuff that is a human. The other compassion-cultivating processes I know of ask me to tackle the whole person ("And now, imagine yourself, the fullness of who you are, resting in a warm, loving light."). There's just too much in that hot mess of humanness to get my compassion around at one time. But Frank showed me how a one-part-of-me-at-a-time approach will steadily and surely bring compassion to an entire being. What a gift.

The second invitation in Frank's teaching — and the tipping point for me — appealed to my sense of adventure. Every time Frank led the Practice, he took me on a journey through an endlessly enthralling landscape. And okay, yes, that landscape was all about me, the landscape of my interior world. But what could be more intriguing? Or more exciting? Or more full of fascinating and useful discoveries? Exactly. I've explored Hezbollah-held areas of Lebanon, exchanged stories of family tragedies with a government spy in Zimbabwe, driven through lava-filled black rain from a volcanic eruption in Guatemala, been unexpectedly left to fend for myself in the sands of a Jordanian desert, joined in night-time anti-gun walks through crime-ridden U.S. neighborhoods, and paraglided off of Southern California cliffs (the most unnerving thing on this list). Each of those and other experiences beyond my comfort zone taught me something new and valuable about myself, human beings, and life in the world. So surely I could face a Frank-guided, compassion-filled journey into the terrifying landscape of my interior world. Couldn't I? Yes, I could. Yes, I have. What a trip.

Finally, I cannot end this tribute without a nod to what Frank has taught me about hope in the midst of hopelessness. In all he says and does, Frank teaches resurrection through crucifixion. But he doesn't use traditional Christian theological language. Instead, he talks about "searching for gold in the crap." And Frank's life offers a master course in finding that gold. When it seems appropriate to tell his own story — that is, when it seems that speaking of his wounds might help others heal — Frank will describe his path through childhood sexual abuse, the emotional traumas that flowed from that into his adulthood, and his unrelenting spiritual search for stability and health.

That quest for wholeness does not end. It cannot end, for Frank or for any of us, if our world carries any measure of pain at all. And so Frank, in his life and work, will continue to show us how we can find healing and freedom for ourselves and for others. He will continue to describe for us the intricacies of human experience. He will always tell us in stories, teachings, and companionship that we, too, can become passionate, compassionate people for ourselves, for others, for the world. And yet, and yet…exactly how do we do that, Frank? Can you boil that down for us?

Ah yes. How, indeed. Hear again the teacher's words in a form that has stuck with me, a version rarely voiced and eternally accurate: "The only way to bring real freedom, real healing, real compassion to the world is to find the place of the deepest pain, the most profound brokenness. And then you work with that. You work with the shit. Because, the truth is, that's where the flowers grow."

That's Frank's story. (At least as I remember it.) And I'm sticking to it.

Afterword: An Invitation...

Eric Kyle

Inward. Upward. Outward. These are the three movements of the Spirit that were cultivated in me as one of Frank's doctoral students at the Claremont School of Theology. It is these three movements that we were taught the Divine Creator continually strives to work through as the Spirit transforms our world. It is these three movements that, as so eloquently stated by Frank in the Epigraph, are harmonic rhythms that heal, restore, and propel creation forward. Yet, it takes our participation in these movements in order for a planet of justice, love, equity, inclusion, and compassion to continue to evolve. It requires our active responsiveness to these three holy movements of God.

This text is one act of responsiveness to these movements as inspired and guided by the life and work of Frank. Each chapter illustrates how the Divine has worked through Frank's teaching, scholarship, and service to motivate these authors as we have been blessed by Frank: Inwardly, Upwardly, and Outwardly. Some of these chapters have focused on the intense inward journey that Frank or themselves have engaged and blossomed through. Other chapters provided examples of how Frank's mentoring has upwardly inspired the authors toward greater fulfillment of their own calling. Still other chapters demonstrate the outwardly and continually evolving applications of Frank's theories and practices to their own vocations. Through time and across cultures, the Spirit has continued to bless and guide each of us through Frank's impact on our lives.

As someone who was deeply formed by Frank's mentoring, however, I know that it has never been about Frank, or even what God is doing with and through him. Rather, Frank's vocation has long focused on empowering others to connect with the Divine within and among themselves. And so, in this Afterword, I believe that God is offering each of us an invitation. It is the Eternal Invitation that ever-exists in every moment, in each particle of creation, in each emergent whole. It is the invitation to engage in these three movements with the Spirit and discern God's calling for us to be and become with the Divine in the Eternal Now.

179

As highlighted in my chapter, in their paper, "Contemplative Race Theory," Cohen and Carter explore the use of the Compassion Practice to help teach about race and racism.[6] As it has been developed by the Center for Engaged Compassion, Carter outlines the following steps for the Compassion Practice:

- Anchoring: This step fosters a grounded, non-reactive, non-judgmental space that the practitioner can dwell in and return to if needed throughout the practice. Anchoring is used to create this space via focusing on one's breath, the weightiness of one's body, or imagining oneself in a space that elicits feelings of safety, compassion, or sacredness.

- Beholding: From this grounded space practitioners are invited to notice the presence of difficult feelings or negative voices which are then imaginally placed in a separate space where they can be observed and examined. Beholding fosters a sense of open curiosity and allows interior freedom to emerge.

- Connecting: Deepens one's experience with the feeling or voice being examined through an imaginal process of personifying it, usually as a small misunderstood child. This enables the practitioner to converse with the feeling or voice and allows a relationship with him or her to emerge. The process of connecting fosters empathic care, compassion, wisdom about what the feeling or voice needs, and the beginnings of interior freedom toward the feeling or voice being examined.

- Dwelling: As the feeling or voice becomes more understood and a sense of compassion begins to grow, practitioners are now encouraged to invite the source of that compassion to engage the child as well as themselves in a healing and restorative way. Dwelling fosters interior freedom, a widening sense of interior stillness, an experience of communion or union, and an encompassing feeling of compassion.

- Embracing your Restored Self: In the penultimate step of the compassion practice participants are asked to notice what

---

6 Seth Schoen and Christopher Carter, "Contemplative Race Theory," in *Association for Contemplative Mind in Higher Education (ACMHE)* (Amherst, MA2013). http://www.contemplativemind.org/files/ConRaceTheory_PUB_Draft.pdf

grace they are receiving within it and to let it soak into them and claim it as a living part of who they are. This step fosters interior stability, wisdom, and a new experiential awareness of one's reality.

- Freely Discerning Compassionate Action: From this state of compassion and in-dwelling grace practitioners are guided to shift their attention to the original feeling or voice with which they began the practice. Beholding it with empowered compassion they are invited to sense within themselves a way to engage that feeling or voice that embodies the compassion and grace they have experienced during the practice. This final step turns empathy and wisdom into empowered compassionate action or behavior.

As you complete this book, I invite you to return to its beginning, before you opened its pages. I invite you retrace your journey through these chapters by following the steps as outlined by Cohen and Carter. Allow yourself inwardly recall the thoughts, feelings, and bodily sensations that arose within you as you turned each page, encountered each idea, were swept away by each story. Notice at which points parts of you were lifted upwardly to new heights, experienced sharp drops into doldrums, or were moved to set the book down and engage outwardly in some type of action. As you reflect on the myriad ways that the chapters of this book has moved parts of you, Anchor yourself in the Divine and Behold these movements with curiosity. Allow yourself to Connect more deeply with the Sacred in some of these movements, Dwelling deeply with the ones through which God seems to be inviting you towards.

As you contemplate these deeper movements, where are you discovering and finding parts of yourself embracing new versions of a Restored Self? Where are you being uplifted and empowered as a beautiful manifestation of the Divine? Where are feelings being nudged to engage with yourself, the people and communities you are connected to, and the wider world in new and different ways - ways that bend towards justice, inclusion, and Compassionate Action? I encourage you to abide deeply and longingly with these Inward, Upward, and Outward movements; to discern communally with them; to follow them as counseled by experienced spiritual companions. For in doing so, as has been my experience in being mentored by Frank for many years, you may very well find yourself connecting ever more deeply with the very Pulse of Life: the Divine within, to, and beyond all that is, has been, and is yet to be…

About the Authors

Dr. Alane Daugherty is a writer, speaker, and professor. Her work focuses on teaching people how to transform chaotic and limiting emotional patterns to ones that are self-affirming, life enhancing, and truly transformative. She is the author of Unstressed: How Somatic Awareness Can Transform Your Body's Stress Response and Build Emotional Resilience from New Harbinger Publications, From Mindfulness to Heartfulness: A Journey of Transformation through the Science of Embodiment from Balboa Press, The Power Within: From Neuroscience to Transformation from Kendall Hunt Publishers and De-stress with Dr. Alane - an Audio meditation CD available on Amazon and iTunes. Dr. Daugherty's passion, professional training, research, and teaching experience are grounded in the neuroscience of transformation, emotional literacy and the importance of the mind/body/spirit dynamic.

Andrew Dreitcer, Ph.D., is Dean, Professor of Spirituality, Co-Director of the Center for Engaged Compassion, Claremont School of Theology. His work focuses on interreligious comparative explorations of how spiritual practices form lives of compassion. Andrew has co-led workshops on compassion and justice in Zimbabwe, the US, and the UK. Church-based community activism and a year at the Christian monastery have shaped his spiritual life. His book 'Living Compassion -- Loving Like' Jesus was named one of the "Best Books of 2017" by the website 'Spirituality and Practice.'

Rev. Dr. Nancy Fowler earned her Ph.D. in spiritual formation at Claremont School of Theology, graduating in 2020. Frank Rogers was her advisor. Her son struggled with mental health issues for his entire life and finally chose to end his life when he was 24. Through her studies, she discovered that Rogers' Compassion Practice helped to bring some comfort and solace to her deep grief. She feels called to bring this program to others who are dealing with life issues. She is a member of Pacific Beach Christian Church (DOC) and is on the leadership team for Beloved Way and its non-profit offshoot, Beloved Compassion Network. She lives in San Diego with her husband and daughter.

Rev. Dr. Mark Chung Hearn, Ph.D., is Associate Dean of Academic Affairs at Church Divinity School of the Pacific in Berkeley, CA. He was a teaching assistant and studied with Frank Rogers Jr. at Claremont School of Theology in Practical Theology with an emphasis in Religious Education and Spiritual Formation.

Natasha Huang is a firstborn daughter to immigrants from Taiwan. Natasha has lived in/near cities like Los Angeles, Taipei, San Francisco, New Haven, Boston, and Philadelphia. She graduated from Claremont School of Theology with a Ph.D. in Education and Formation. Her beloved community consists of intercultural, international, interfaith, and intergenerational friendships. A lover of soccer, swing dancing, dogs, hikes, naps, yoga, and swimming, Natasha is also fluent in Mandarin, a board-certified Music Therapist, and an experienced violin teacher. Natasha currently works as a chaplain educator at the hospital where her brother was born.

Joung Hee Kim earned her Ph.D. in spiritual formation at Claremont School of Theology. She has been formed by Dr. Frank Rogers Jr.'s teaching, spirituality, and character since her master's degree program in 2013. Dr. Kim lives in Korea, teaching Christian spirituality at Hanil University & Presbyterian Theological Seminary and Torch Trinity Graduate University. Her teaching and studies focus on Christian spirituality, spiritual formation and direction, and Compassion Practice. She translated Dr. Rogers' Compassion in Practice into Korean, and her vision is to establish a branch of the Center for Engaged Compassion in Korea.

Sheryl A. Kujawa-Holbrook, EdD, PhD, is a priest of the Episcopal Diocese of Los Angeles, historian, editor, writer, religious educator, retreat leader, and pastoral/practical theologian. She has published widely, including books, articles, chapters, and reviews. Kujawa-Holbrook currently serves as professor of practical theology at Claremont School of Theology, and professor of Anglican Studies at

Bloy House, the Episcopal Theological School at Los Angeles. A fellow of the Royal Historical Society, Kujawa-Holbrook is editor-in-chief of Anglican and Episcopal History, pastoral theology review editor for Anglican Theological Review, and board member for the journal Magistra. A theological educator for nearly forty years, Kujawa-Holbrook is the former vice president for academic affairs and dean of the faculty at Claremont School of Theology, and the former academic dean and Suzanne Radley Hiatt professor of feminist pastoral theology and church history at the Episcopal Divinity School.

Eric Kyle, Ph.D., is Director of the 21st Century Pedagogy Institute (21CPI) at the University of Central Oklahoma. His teaching, scholarship, and service focus on the intersection of the following three areas: 1) Faculty Development; 2) Peace Education; and 3) Teaching Religion & Theology. Eric has published several books, including: Living Spiritual Praxis, Sacred Systems, Spiritual Being & Becoming, and Educating in the Spirit. As a graduate of the Claremont School of Theology, Kyle continues to integrate contemplative practices into each of these areas.

Cate Wilson, Ph.D., is an interdisciplinary scholar of engaged compassion, contemplative practices, nonviolent communication, and interpersonal neurophysiology. From this multi-dimensional base and her passion for elevating female-identifying individuals, she developed, "The Goddess Finishing School," a program to empower and uplift those who identify as girls and women—in mind, body, and spirit. Cate draws on 15 years of experience as a line-producer and production manager in the film and television industries for her work guiding individuals and organizations through systems thinking, organizational development, and long-term planning. She currently serves as Manager of Organizational Engagement and Strategic Partnerships at USC Shoah Foundation where she works with partners around the globe.

Aizaiah G. Yong, Ph.D., currently serves as Associate Dean of Students and Assistant Professor of Spirituality at the Claremont School of Theology teaching classes related to practical theology,

185

trauma studies, spirituality and mysticism, and interreligious leadership. He has completed training to be a recognized facilitator in the practice of Engaged Compassion, mindful anti-racist leadership, and is also a level two Internal Family Systems Practitioner. His latest book, Multiracial Cosmotheandrism: A Practical Theology of Multiracial Experiences (Orbis Books) received the highly distinguished international 2022 Raimon Panikkar Prize and critically considers how the lives and spiritual experiences of mixed-race people can transform efforts towards racial and planetary justice.

Index

188

feelings, feeling, 21, 32, 46, 56, 114, 115, 140, 152, 153, 158, 170, 177, 180, 181

Form, 18, 80, 82, 89, 93, 98, 100, 101, 106, 144, 161, 175, 178

Formation: 8, 41, 52, 82, 83, 116, 118, 120, 121, 128, 172, 177, spiritual -, iii, 1, 52, 87, 117, 144, 166, 169, 172, transformation, 4, 21, 33, 57, 58, 65, 70, 79, 107, 134, 149, 150, 166, 168

Freedom, 12, 14, 15, 16, 17, 18, 32, 81, 84, 85, 155, 157, 162, 168, 169, 172, 173, 175, 178, 180

Georgia, 20

god, 11, 14, 77, 78, 79, 80, 81, 82, 87, 88, 94, 95, 96, 99, 100, 101, 102, 105, 107, 108, 109, 112, 145, 165, 179, 181

goddess: - School, 111, 116-118, 120-128

The God of Shattered Glass (Rogers Jr.), 77

Golden Rule, 84

Grande, Sandy, 23

Grief, 3, 42, 44, 50, 54, 115, 141, 142-145, 147, 163

Grounded, 1, Grounding, 15, 33, 122, 141, 175

Haiku, 43

Harmony, 11

Healing, 2, 11, 32, 35, 36, 42, 44, 47, 52, 57, 61, 63, 64, 66, 72, 73, 77, 78, 81-84, 86-91, 139, 143, 147-150, 156, 158-163, 166, 170, 173-175, 178

Heaven: 94, 97, 104, kingdom of - , 93, 94, 102, 104, 105-106, 109

Heteronormativity, 30

Hope, 11

Hospitality, 69, 96, 111, 116-117, 119, 124, 125, 126

Human subjectivity, 10

Identify, 16, 17, 58, 66, 92, 93, 104, 122, 158, 160, 171, 173, 175, female-identifying, 111, 116, 121, 127-129

Identity: 5, 6, 15, 17, 18, 28, 41, 45-49, 128, - formation, 41, 49, 55, 82, 121, 128

Ignatian spirituality, 11

Imagery, 157, 159-163

Immigrants: Honduran, 20

Imposter Syndrome, 9

Integrity, 15

Integration, 41

Interior, 32, 33, 67, 85, 102, 104, 105, 106, 11, 114, 115, 116, 117, 124, 161, 177, 178, 180, 181, interiority, 1, 2, 67, 68, internal, 10, 12, 14, 16, 17, 18, 63, 84, 116, 125, 128, 141, 149, 150, 161, 162, Inward, 85, 92, 95, 104, 105, 108, 109, 118, 179, 181

Internalized Oppression, 31

Internal Family Systems, iii, 2, 41, 42, 51, 54, 55, 131, 133, 143: Exiles, 42, Protectors, 42, Parts, 42

Interreligious Engagement, 82

Intersectionality, 20

Intersectional Pedagogy: Creative Education Practices for Gender and Peace Work, (Harmat), 21

St. Iraeneus, 14

Jesus, 59, 62, 69, 86, 87, 89, 94, 102-105, 107, 113, 132, 176

Jesus Christ, 62n18, 92, 101, 102, 104

Journey, 10, 13, 14, 16, 45, 47, 61, 63, 77, 92, 94-100, 102, 104-106, 108-109, 144, 147-150, 162, 177-179, 181

Judaism, 83

Korean American, 8, 103: eldership, 8, women, 81

Lament, 44

Learning the Way of Peace (UNESCO), 21

Living Human Document, 45

Love, 10, 12, 21, 33, 43, 55, 84, 86, 87, 89, 95, 102, 104, 113, 122, 139, 153, 158, 161, 163   loving, 1, 9, 67, 68, 79, 85, 87, 89, 90, 92, 102, 103, 105, 107, 108, 109, 113, 114, 147, 153, 156, 177 - kindness, 112

Memory, 6, 17, 43, 149, 151, 153-162

Mentorship, 8

Methodism, 20: Social Principles, 20

Mitchell, Tania D., 27

Critical Mixed Race Studies, 63

Movement, 1, 9, 13, 17, 70, 71, 88, 107, 108, 161, 162, 171, 175

Multiplicity, 15

Nationalism, 28

Narcissism, 17

Narrative: 5-6,: Literacy, 41, Pedagogy, 81, Psychology, 15, theory, 5-6

Nature, 50, 83, 101, 106-107, 141, 151, 162

Neuger, Christine Cozad, 81

Made in the USA
Monee, IL
22 September 2023

43194078R00116